FASHION 2.0:

BLOGGING YOUR WAY
TO THE FRONT ROW

THE INSIDER'S GUIDE TO TURNING YOUR FASHION BLOG INTO

A PROFITABLE BUSINESS AND LAUNCHING A NEW CAREER

YULI ZIV

ISBN: 978-1463611385

Visit www.YuliZiv.com for more info.

Prosperity, prosperity, prosperity is perpetual with people who prefer to be penetrating, prepared and purposeful. But prosperity only comes to those who are trustworthy, deliver, and are content and consistent. Basically, it boils down to commitment. If you put your soul into anything, you can plug into the whole world. It will be yours. You can sweep prosperity with your commitment. Contain, commit, and be continuous.

~Yogi Bhajan

Contents

Chapter 3: Relationships

Chapter 4: Revenue

Editor's Letter.

I, like many of you, am a blogger.

I, like many of you, have looked at other bloggers who seem to have more than I have. Larger-scale relationships, partnerships with desirable brands, financial rewards for doing what they love best in a format that is revolutionizing the way we communicate and relate to each other and fashion. We all want a bigger slice of the pie.

The question is: how do you get it?

As the person who was honored to read and edit this manuscript, I will tell you that this book you're holding is one of the best ways to start. Written in an honest, forthright manner, Yuli gives you heaps of insider information from one of the most respected perspectives in our industry: hers. She's not just spouting statistics. Yuli is known as one of the strongest, most knowledgeable talents in the fashion blogging field and she knows the ins and outs and the playbook to success from both sides.

As a blogger, she's one of the most respected in the field and as a business woman, her talents and abilities are almost unmatched. Style Coalition was the first partnership between a major print fashion magazine and the blogging community. While others will claim to have invented the wheel, Yuli did, in fact, invent that one. The advice you're reading is from her own personal experience and the inside information that she's shared with many of the best in the industry. In short, it's the "how" you've been looking for from someone who's done it. Now, she's going to tell you how to do it for yourself.

I tell you this as a fellow blogger, someone who works tirelessly to gather information for my readers and to give them my own strong, personal perspective on what it takes to feel and look their absolute best. Reading this book has given me the opportunity to apply many of its tips and tricks and every single one of them—*every single one*—has increased traffic, profitability and has garnered me relationships with my dream list of brands. I offered to edit the book because I believed in what she was trying to do. I took the advice in this book because I knew it would pay off... and has it ever paid off.

I encourage you to read through the book once or twice. Highlight things and come back to them. Do the exercises no matter how long it takes you. Inevitably, you will see results.

This is your blog. This is your future and this is your chance to make it to the front row. I'll see you there.

All the best,

Kristin Booker

Editor/Publisher

Fashion.Style.Beauty

Introduction.

The reason I wrote this book was because I have a desire to ignite your creative entrepreneurial spirit, inspire you and give you tactical advice to help turn your passion for blogging into a successful business. I believe it's more realistic than ever to build a full-time career as a blogger, particularly in the fashion and lifestyle vertical.

This book is written from the point of view of my personal, hands-on experience in this particular arena. First as a social media expert and blogger and, most recently, as the Founder & CEO of Style Coalition, where I have been helping bloggers to earn a living doing what they love.

This isn't your typical Blogging 101 read, but rather a deeper look into blogging as a business. There are a large number of great books covering the basics of the blogging craft, which I'm happy to recommend in the resources section at the end of this book. The journey you and I will take together in this book utilizes my years of experience and will help you create a valuable blogging strategy. This launch plan will give you the tools and skills you will need to turn your ideas into a valuable, profitable business.

With the rise of Twitter and the pressure to condense information into 140 characters or less, holding your valuable attention might be a tad challenging. Therefore, I made this book as condensed as possible, replacing the descriptive tone with a more direct approach focusing on a call to action. Expect to be motivated, educated and inspired by myself and some power blogger contributors.

It's been my experience that even though there are a large number of books covering blogging basics, such as choosing the right blogging platform, I haven't found many that speak to the professional and business aspects of our new occupation. That's one of the main reasons I wrote this book. We are, after all, business people and we can expect to make money from these valuable media properties. It's no longer just a hobby to work on in your pajamas. If you desire to turn your passion into a real money-making business, this book is for you.

In the past few years, the fashion industry has been seriously shaken up by a new generation of influencers: the bloggers. We've broken the old hierarchy rules, taken front row seats at runway shows and are now poised to take a large piece of the major marketing and advertising budgets from industry-leading brands. Every year, we see more dollars shifted into social media and celebrity endorsements replaced by user-generated recommendations. Bloggers are, in short, a force to be reckoned with and we show no signs of slowing down.

Bloggers are leading the social media revolution and represent the new generation of influencers and content curators. We have risen to power and influence completely on our own, and, unlike traditional print editors, have the freedom to create our own path and build our own careers. We answer to no devil in Prada; we carve our own path, set our own hours and have the ability to live our lives as we see fit. If used correctly, this powerful position in which we find ourselves as online media puts us in the right place at the right time to demand a considerable amount of compensation, power and authority. We just have to be intelligent about the way we go about it.

Being an independent publisher certainly has its advantages, but it also presents many challenges, especially when it comes to positioning your brand and building valuable relationships, the basis for strong business operations and revenue generation. We'll address all of those questions together and help you position yourself as a power-playing, strong professional who will eventually rise high on the influence chain and not only take over the front row of runway shows, but the front row of this industry as a whole.

Also, despite its title, I believe this book can benefit and inspire bloggers in other industries and help them navigate their way to business success in this new post-digital-revolution environment. While we speak of the fashion and lifestyle vertical here, the practice of being a smart and valuable online business person knows no particular vertical. We can all benefit from best practices.

There is nothing I want more than each one of you, the readers, to succeed in realizing your passion and to be out there creating meaningful virtual sources of inspiration for others. I have poured a decade of vast experience into the pages you are about to read and have added valuable insight from some of our industry's top bloggers at the end of each chapter. It is my sincere hope that this combined experience and advice will position each of you to become the next big thing, blogging your way to the front row and beyond. There's no limit to what you can accomplish.

With that said, what are we waiting for? Your front row seat awaits you. Let's help you get there.

My Short Story.

Being an immigrant has been a major defining factor of my entrepreneurial spirit. It's taught me one key thing: the ability to quickly adapt to new conditions.

My family left Communist Russia when I was 15 with just four suitcases (one for each family member) and $1,000 in hand, landing in post-Gulf War Israel in 1991. Our new home created the need for me to become financially independent of my parents, so I was forced to create my own income from a very early age (partially so I could afford the Levi's 501 jeans that were the "uniform" in my high school). When I turned 18, I was forced to serve in the Israeli Defense Forces, as all citizens of the country are mandated to do by law for what seemed like the longest two years of my life. Besides learning useless skills such as how to operate guns, I learned never to trust the path someone had chosen for me and to create my own path in life. Thus, at the age of 27, I took the same suitcase that brought me from Russia and moved even further away—to America, Land of Dreams.

Within three years and with a considerable amount of hard work, I had a green card and my dream job with a corner office at one of New York City's biggest digital marketing agencies. That's when I knew it was time for a new dream, something even more unattainable and challenging—something like conquering the fashion industry. In 2007, I quit my executive job and launched MyItThings.com, a fashion community and blog where readers could share everything from style advice to their favorite new shopping finds. I had a business partner and $10,000 of savings as an initial investment between the two of us for our new venture, but I didn't have a clue about what it meant to run a business and even less of a clue about how we would make money. It took three long years until we saw any income from my entrepreneurial endeavors, but the lessons I learned on my way to that level of success and beyond could not have been more valuable.

In the past two years, I have focused most of my energy on founding and running Style Coalition, a network of fashion and beauty bloggers that today boasts more than 2 million monthly unique visitors and a partnership with one of the most respected fashion magazines in the world—*ELLE*. The ultimate mission of Style Coalition is to help bloggers create revenue channels and turn their blogs into successful and profitable businesses.

As I have watched bloggers rise to the top of the industry, there couldn't be a more perfect time to put everything I have witnessed, experienced and learned into a guide for success: this book. Parts of it began as posts on my business blog, yuliziv.com, and the overwhelming response I received for the insight and advice I've written has convinced me there is a substantial audience who can benefit from my first-hand experience in helping bloggers turn their dreams into a profitable business.

So here we are. Let's begin the journey of helping you to turn your passion for blogging into a lucrative success.

Chapter 1: Planning

Most people can be divided into two groups: those who are passively living life waiting for opportunities to come their way, and those who are actually out there working, actively planning their successes.

If you fall into the latter category—those who know what they want, where you're going and have some ideas on how to get there—you'll need a plan. This is where the concept of planning becomes crucial. You don't need to know all the exact details (there could be multiple ways to achieve what you want), but if you don't have a plan to get where you are going, how will you ever get there?

This chapter will help you define what you want out of your blogging career and plan the crucial next steps on your way to success.

Make a Commitment.

Commitment is absolutely the most important thing for any new venture you start. Ask yourself: will I be able to commit to it fully for a long period of time? This concept might sound easy, but I see many people underestimate the power of commitment, jumping from one idea to another, from one blog to another, from one branding strategy to another, lacking the commitment it takes to see any of these ventures come to any level of real success. The truth is that every single idea in this world has a chance to succeed; every single blog has a chance to become the most-read blog in its category if only enough time is spent researching, building, optimizing and eventually monetizing it. Yes, it might change visually and textually, but if you are committed to the core idea of your blog, you will find a way to make it work.

Commitment is more than just saying, "I will do this." Some deeper steps are involved.

Steps to commitment:

1. Start by creating a personal brand that aligns deeply with your personal values, one that you can commit to for a long period of time. Ensure that it doesn't reflect a passing trend or your current stage of life. It should be something you can realistically see yourself doing—and enjoying—five or more years from now.

2. Decide upon the amount of energy and time (daily, weekly, and monthly) you are really willing to put into making your blog a success.

3. Decide on the amount of money you are willing to invest in building your business. This doesn't have to be a huge investment as there are certain online tools that can make blogging as cost effective as possible, but you will have to invest some amount of money as well as the value of your time. There are al-

ways costs to starting a business, no matter how small. You will need to plan and budget for these expenses.

Once you have committed to these simple steps, make yourself accountable for your own success. It's easy to come up with excuses as to why something didn't work; it's much harder to commit to pouring all your energy into making something work. Don't get me wrong. I myself have historically suffered from lack of commitment as an entrepreneur and blogger, but what I have found is that when I stick to something long enough and remain persistent, it usually works.

We are so used to a fast-paced reality online, where trends change so quickly, companies come and go, and users are always on the hunt for the next big thing. However, if you look at the most successful blogs out there, it took them years to get where they are. Most successful bloggers' bios speak to the years it took them to achieve the success (and sometimes many failures) that got them where they are today.

When people ask me how is it that I succeeded at X and/or Y, my answer is usually that I've been persistent and have been doing it long enough to make it work. I've sacrificed my sleep, my financial savings and sometimes even my personal life because at that moment my idea was the most important thing to me. I've spent over ten years building my career in the online media industry in various roles—with four of them on my own as an entrepreneur. It's a long time period by any measure, but this is the choice I've made. I've committed to my business like most people commit to a marriage or a family. Dedication is the name of the game to achieving any level of success.

This doesn't mean you have to wait for years until you become successful. I see amazing new blogs popping up every year and changing the game. But not every idea is brilliant, and some require patience to develop. You must keep fine-tuning your idea until you find your voice, your readers, and the things that get the most responses. In most cases, testing and researching takes time. Sometimes weeks, months or years will pass until you manage to turn your passion into a business, but remember not to get discouraged in the meantime. It's not all about the end result.

When you are committed to something, you see the bad and good as part of the process and learn to enjoy the journey to success with all of its ups and downs equally. You will notice how the low points become inspiration for new and better things to come.

In December 2009, I had zero dollars in my business bank account, and my co-founder who built the site with me from scratch announced he was leaving the company for a "normal" job. I was devastated. At that point, we had run through all our savings and invested 110% of our energy in this venture, but unfortunately, the site wasn't giving the expected return at the time, causing my business partner to lose faith. Closing the business and going back to the corporate world seemed like the next logical step, but something in me believed that this whole experience couldn't possibly be all for nothing. I was committed to making it work.

That's when I turned into my own top salesperson. I spent days and weeks cold-calling companies and offering them advertising and sponsorship on the site without much success. I was nervous before every call, trying to memorize my pitch and work on reducing my foreign accent (Have I mentioned how much I hated sales, especially cold calls?). However, the idea of getting a "normal" job scared me so much that I somehow found the inspiration to do something I didn't even like to bring some hope and future to my fledgling idea. Finally, I was lucky enough to sell a sponsorship package to a long lead publication that we had spoken with a few months prior. Success! That small win brought back all the hope from the beginning of my venture and showed me that my commitment to success was paying off. Later, I even learned to love the sales process and looked at it as an adventure, full of great surprises and great new connections.

Failures are an essential part of the experience and will eventually lead to something bigger and better once you stop looking at them negatively. When you get zero response to certain content or your traffic starts tanking, use it to fuel your creative brain. I can almost guarantee that will be the moment when you will find "your thing"—something inspiring that makes your content unique.

Remain committed to finding that "thing" and evolve it into your personal and professional goals. Don't underestimate this process – it can be a huge step in your business but also in your own self-development, helping you to discover who you are as a person and a creative force. Your blog can be a huge part of this process; capturing your voice in writing can be directly correlated with finding your own voice in life. The experience can not only make you a better online publisher, it can actually make you a stronger, better person.

I've found this realization has been very helpful for me. It caused me to look at blogging not as a silly hobby but as a tool for self-expression, something that forced the inner me to emerge and expose my personality to the world. As a result of this perspective, it has been much easier for me to commit to it. After all, it's easier to commit to a self-development process than a blog development one, isn't it?

Define Your Mission.

Once you are committed to your blog concept and all that it will take to develop it into a success, you must decide upon how your blog will add value to the lives of your readers. If you think about it, all successful businesses have one thing in common: **they bring value to people**. This is the reason they're able to charge their clients a fee for the services they provide. Defining your mission and how you will provide this value is therefore absolutely essential if you're going to become a successful, profitable business.

Your blog can create value for your readers in multiple ways:

- **Inspiration.** It can be as simple as a collection of inspiring visuals or a collection of quotes, thoughts, editorials, metaphors or color palettes. People are constantly looking for their daily fix of fresh new visuals that stimulate their mind. Take Gala from *GalaDarling.com*, who creates daily inspirational posts that may include anything from fashion advice to self-esteem tips and photos for inspiration. Thousands of people, especially teens, are fascinated by her personality and find her lifestyle and visual language simply inspirational. Think about how you can become an inspirational source. Even though you might not produce all the content, you can curate it.

- **Practical advice.** I see more and more niche blogs reaching success by focusing on practical advice that appeals to and captures a certain audience. Take Kelly from *Alterations-Needed.com*, who gives valuable tips to petite women on how to adjust their clothing to better fit and flatter their bodies. You would be surprised how many women need this type of advice in their lives! Kelly's blog is full of detailed tips and photographs that can make any petite woman look her absolute best.

- **Conversation.** Don't look at your blog solely as a platform to push content but as a place for meaningful conversation. Consider how you can build a community around a specific subject that will bring your readers together to converse on a daily basis. Kat from *Corporette.com* manages to bring thousands of readers to her site daily by creating interesting conversations among corporate women—lawyers, bankers, etc.—who want to look fashionable but have the challenge of complying with their job's "dress code." Every single post on Kat's blog turns into a lively discussion, making it the ultimate community for fashionable, professional women.

All of these examples show how important (and lucrative) it is to provide value to others in order to succeed. It's important for your blog, and it's even more important for your own life. What is it that you are trying to achieve with your life and how can others benefit from that personal mission? Answer this question for yourself first and then see how that can be incorporated into the goal of your blog. It can be as simple as, *"I want to become a joyful person and spread my joy around. The mission of my blog is to become a daily source of joy for people,"* to something more complex like, *"I want to educate people about subject X because it's close to my heart for reason Y. My blog is a great step towards accomplishing that mission."*

See how this one step takes the simple musings of a blogger to someone who actually inspires, helps to educate and fosters positive social interactions? It's a powerful exercise. Do not skip this step.

Be sure to outline your mission on your blog in a prominent place where everyone can see it. You will get respect from your readers and will even gain some new ones once people see you are a mission-driven individual and not just someone who uses their online property as a void in which to project their random thoughts and ideas.

Always consider the meaning of everything you produce in life—be it content, material products or thoughts. Think about how it falls into the larger scope of your own life and the world around you. Sometimes, the ease of opening a blog or producing content online can mislead us and allow us to put meaningless content that's not quite thought through. Refer to your blog as a public space for which you are personally responsible and make sure it fulfills your mission. It should be a clear and unique representation of who you are and the value you provide.

Align Your Personal Goals.

Now that you've decided on your larger mission, take time to align it with your life and personal goals. This is a crucial step because it keeps you personally invested and committed for a much longer period of time. If you've spent years building a certain expertise, try to see how your blog can showcase some of it. Look at your résumé and career path and see how your blog fits into it—or creates a whole new path.

It's time to review all of your assets and see how they will best work to your advantage—everything from your personality, body type, style, education, place of birth, work history and hobbies—and ask yourself two very simple but very important questions:

- **How will my blog represent who I am?**

- **How will my blog influence my career path?**

The first question is crucial to everything you do, especially with the new media property (blog) you are creating. Many people in the industry will associate your own personal brand and personality with your blog from now on. Do these two go hand-in-hand? They should. Does your blog look authentic and sincere? It must.

Here's an example of using your "assets" to your advantage: If you are a plus-sized woman, you might be very helpful to other women by making it the focus of your blog. Why? Because you will have more personal experiences with shopping the plus-sized category than anyone else, adding valuable insight and advice that others without that experience could possibly provide. You can share your frustrations, incite positive change and even give savvy tips on how to look and feel your absolute best. That would create a passionate readership that would come to rely upon your expertise and personal insight. On the other hand, if you are a plus-sized woman blogging only about stick-thin models and their seemingly fabulous lives, this might come across as unauthentic and confuse your readers. They will most likely leave your blog to follow someone else who is able to provide a more authentic vision and voice they can relate to, leaving you with a declining readership. Why not capture and keep people based on what you know best?

Consider another example: if you've had experience working at a vintage store, you probably know a lot about it. Vintage is a huge component and influence in today's fashion as, in my opinion, there are less places for trends and more room for expression of personal style which combines pieces from all eras. Don't be afraid to get too niche. How about analyzing today's fashion from the vintage point of view? You can decide if something has a potential to last decades and become vintage. Even in the vintage niche, there are various subjects on which you could potentially focus and define yourself as an expert.

Get a piece of paper and a pen and try to define yourself in a few keywords, then see if these keywords can define your blog as well. If you see any disconnect between the two, try to think why that may be. You might find some deeper issues surfacing among these disparities, such as body image, personal insecurities and lack of acceptance of who you really are. This can later stand in your way on the road to success, so it's better to see a clear picture of yourself and how your blog is representing these factors from the very beginning. Look for solutions to any differences that impact your ability to be authentic early on so they can cease to become road blocks to your inevitable success. Some of the best bloggers live the way they write and follow their own advice.

If you can't draw a line between your current job, lifestyle, and personality and your blog, think about what stands behind this desire for a new, completely different adventure. Is your blog some sort of escape from reality? Then what are you trying to escape from? If you live in a small town where people could not care less about fashion, and your daily job couldn't be more removed from the glitz and glamour of a fashion magazine editor, think about why you want to write a fashion blog and how your demographic might affect it. It can be very useful when building your audience and readership. Perhaps you can think of more people who would love to escape their world with you. Try to define who they might be and what would be the best way to write for them. Make your small town origin an asset and use it as a point of view to your blog.

Even though your blog can be a completely new chapter in your life and a career-changing experience, you will have a stronger advantage integrating some of your existing expertise into your new venture. If you majored in Art History during college, your fashion blog could potentially be built around comparisons of fashion and art in different historical periods, adding more expert credit and depth to your content. It's good to try new things and new directions, but you will be twice as smart as your competitor when you bring another layer of knowledge to the table.

I subscribe to the theory that everything you do in life somehow helps you to continue along your own path, even though it's hard to see how at times. If you are aware of this concept and try to act consciously, you have a huge advantage over others who don't. Going back to our examples, Kat from *Corporette.com* couldn't be as successful and authoritative as she is in her niche if she wasn't a lawyer herself. In fact, she started a blog as a way to share her love of fashion and open discussions with women who are just like her and face similar challenges. Her blog is a direct continuation of her career, even though it's hard to see a connection between corporate law and fashion blogging at first.

This is just one example of how using all of your assets and experiences paired with aligning your blog with those winning capabilities can lead to incredible successes. Every single piece of your life can be a starting point, an inspiration and something that eventually leads to a long-term career and personal fulfillment.

Create a Business Plan.

Now that you are inspired and clear on your personal and professional goals, it's time to take the next step and define your business goals.

If the words "business plan" make your creative persona cringe, please stay with me! I promise to not bore you with big marketing clichés and unknown financial terms.

After building two businesses and scratching business plans on at least five more, I can confidently say that having some version of a business plan definitely helps.

Let me break some common misconceptions about business plans to make it more fun:

- **Business plans don't have to be written for external use.** Think about it as a road map guiding your blog. No one but you ever has to see it, so take some of the pressure off.

- **Don't worry about the language or using proper fancy business terms.** This is where the content is more important than the package. Write it in a tone that is funny, quirky, cynical, grandiose, or silly. Whatever makes it the most fun and helpful for you, do it, because it's about *you*, not anyone else.

- **Don't be afraid to make unrealistic goals or expectations.** No one else is judging you or comparing your projections at the end of the year. Let your desires go wild and put them on paper. Big successes start with big dreams.

Now that you are feeling less stressed about this process, let's look at some of the key parts you must define for your blog using an illustrative example—a fake blog called CampusStyleSaturdays.com:

1. **Mission statement.** We've already talked about it briefly, but simply put, this explains why your blog exists. Let's say the plan

for your blog will focus on outfit ideas for a Saturday night targeted toward college girls. Here is the short business plan for the blog: "CampusStyleSaturdays.com is a style advice blog that aims to help college girls who would love to dress fashionably every Saturday night, but can't afford the latest runway looks on the salary of a library assistant."

2. **Business concept.** What's the value proposition for both your readers and potential advertisers or sponsors? Example: "CampusStyleSaturdays.com is the ultimate destination for college girls, which makes it extremely appealing for certain budget brands favored by young women, like H&M, looking to expose their products to this particular customer."

3. **Target market**. Describe your readers, their needs, and what value your blog might bring to them. For example: "College girls are extremely competitive about fashion and want to make sure they always look better than their girlfriends. It's also important to them to have a new outfit every week, even if they can't necessarily afford it."

4. **Primary competitors and their key advantages**. "There are tons of huge sites focusing on college fashion, including X and Y. They have been out there for years; have strong recognizable brands, steady income, multiple writers and a strong following." Research your competitors, note them and describe how and why they rate as competition.

5. **Key competitive capabilities**. Simply describe why you are the best person to run your blog and how your blog is going to beat your competition. "I'm living and breathing the campus life every day and know exactly the challenges college girls are facing. By focusing on a very specific niche and just one day of the week, CampusStyleSaturdays.com attracts readers' attention around a similar problem while creating a community of passio-

nate readers who comment with their own advice. While other blogs are posting throughout the week, CampusStyleSaturdays.com is focusing on becoming the ultimate destination on the most important night of the week, when girls are looking for outfit inspiration the most."

6. **Key weaknesses**. Be honest and list all the things that might stand between you and a huge success. It can be as big as writing skills and as small as lack of online friends who will read your blog in your crucial inaugural phase. "While fashion is my expertise, my writing skills could use some help in finding my own style. To achieve that, I'm planning to: 1) take a writing workshop in the next three months; 2) research other blogs for writing style inspiration; and, 3) test different writing styles on my blog to find out what gets the most responses and clicks."

7. **Strategy**. Outline how you are going to utilize your advantages to build a successful blog and business. Describe how often you will post, what unique features the blog will have, and what will make the readers come back again and again.

8. **Milestones**. Define what milestones will make you proud and keep you motivated to continue, then work towards achieving them. "My major milestones would be: being recommended by fellow bloggers, booking an advertiser, a feature in *Teen Vogue*, a TV appearance on a local channel, a mention on *Gossip Girl*, and publishing a book for college girls." (Remember, dream big!)

9. **Future products/services.** Think what else you could offer your audience in the future, even if you have no idea how you will be able to do that right now. For example, "I would love to have a store section on my blog, where girls could shop for the perfect outfits. I will earn affiliate revenue from the sold goods."

10. **Promotion strategy**. Think about how you are going to pro-
    mote yourself and your blog: commenting on other blogs, reach-
    ing out to reporters who might work on relevant stories and of-
    fering yourself as an expert, attending events, trade shows, run-
    ning contests on your site... the list is endless. "I will create a
    small event on my campus where I will ask the girls to show off
    their perfect Saturday looks and will feature them on CampusS-
    tyleSaturdays.com. That way, they will have a reason to link to it
    from their Facebook pages, which will attract more readers in the
    same demographic."

11. **Revenue strategy.** Look at the common revenue channels for
    bloggers, which include CPM banner ads (flat rate) affiliate or
    CPA links/ads (performance or commission-based) direct prod-
    uct sales, sponsorships and contests, and personal appearances
    and speaking engagements (more on that in the Revenue chap-
    ter.) First decide what revenue channels will work best for your
    blog, and focus on them.

12. **Financials.** Define how much money you will need to get your
    blog off the ground and what kind of funds it will take to reach
    your goals. For example, "In order to make CampusStyleSatur-
    days.com look like a serious blog, I need to buy the domain
    name, hire a designer to create a unique logo, purchase a tem-
    plate, and hire a photographer to take occasional professional
    photos around campus. I have $500 of savings set aside, and I'm
    willing to invest these savings into my dream. In the future, I can
    see more investment needed to help promote my blog and create
    unique content, so I'm willing to set aside $100 every month to
    keep my blog growing."

By doing this simple exercise, you will learn to focus your efforts.
Written words have extra power—having a written plan will help you to
commit to the project.

Develop Your Business Persona.

The combination of creativity with business skills will make you basically unstoppable because this means you can turn any dream into business. This is powerful, no matter what industry you're in. If your industry is blogging, develop your business style just like you develop your personal one. I'm not saying you should start wearing "respectable" suits and become a boring person—quite the opposite. Develop your own style of doing business and it will become part of the assets you possess that will make you stand out in the crowd. (Note the use of the word "style" above.)

My personal business style is quite untraditional and probably wouldn't work in many industries. I like to be direct and tell the truth. I like asking tough questions. I'm completely at peace with rejection. I'm not ashamed to ask, "What's in it for me?" during the first meeting, and I'm not afraid to wear pretty dresses to the most boring corporate boardrooms. It took years to lose the fear and just be myself in a business environment, but once I allowed it to happen, I noticed how much more respect I received from potential partners, clients and anyone I meet for a business coffee.

The most important thing you can ever do in any situation—in business or in life—is to simply be true to yourself. Find your business style, and as long as you keep it professional, people will accept it and will actually come to respect you even more.

That said, there are some simple rules that even I have to follow when keeping it professional.

- **Leave emotions aside.** For me it's the #1 rule. You have to be able to analyze each opportunity for what it's worth and act based on logic and intuition, not necessarily your immediate emotions. Example: You really want to work with brand X because you've loved them since grade school, but the opportunity they've offered you is non-paying, although it should be based on the amount of work they are asking you to do. Your first reaction would be to jump and say "YES!" but the business person in you should realize this might create a bad precedent and reduce the chances of you getting paid by brand X in the future.

The same rule goes for rejection. Example: You were left off the invite list for an amazing event by brand Y, where most of your blogger friends not only had the best time but got to meet the designer in person. Your emotional self feels upset, rejected, and you might swear to never write about brand Y again, even though it's one of your favorites. This is when you should ask yourself an honest question: "What can I do better to make sure I'm not left out next time?" Maybe it was a mistake, and if so, find a polite way to remind the PR contact how much you would love to cover their future events. But if the decision to leave you out was conscious, see how you can work to strengthen your relationship with the brand to make sure you'll be top of the list next time.

- **Get to know the rules.** Just because you're in an untraditional career doesn't mean you are not obligated in some way to know the traditional rules of engagement in order to become a professional and respected business person. The world of business operates like any other society—with protocol, rules and certain customs. Read books. Regularly Google things you don't know. Invite other respected professionals out for coffee and ask them questions. Find mentors you admire and adopt mannerisms and advice to strengthen your business acumen. Do anything you can to understand and learn how your industry works. It will save you lots of time, energy, and will prevent confusions and misunderstandings which may lead to the loss of valuable relationships with potential clients or partners.

- **Learn the legal lingo.** Besides knowing about the basic ways industry works, it's extremely important for anyone working independently to understand basic legal terms, rights and obligations. You can't even imagine how many respected bloggers I've met through my career that have signed legal documents without reading them or understanding what they mean. I know lawyers are expensive these days, so if you don't understand something and can't afford a lawyer, I suggest you: 1) ask the person who created the document to explain the basics in simple terms; 2) Google what you don't understand yourself; or 3) ask a business-savvy someone you trust to review it. (Maybe even do all three if the matter is complicated.) It's enough to know the basics and look for them in every agreement. When signing partnership or work agreements, pay attention to things such as:

  o **Exclusivity.** How does this contract affect your ability to work for other companies?

  o **Rights.** Who owns the rights to your work created under the contract?

  o **Deliverables.** What do you promise to deliver, when, how and how often?

  o **Compensation.** How and when are you getting paid?

  o **Confidentiality.** What are you allowed to talk about?

  If you familiarize yourself with these basic terms, you will learn to recognize them in every single work agreement, which will make negotiations much easier. Eventually, you might not even need a lawyer, or you'll only need them for the really big ticket contract items. You'll be able to handle the basics yourself.

- **Learn to communicate with confidence.** If you want to be taken seriously, talk seriously. You might exude confidence when it comes to posing for a street photographer photo, but if you can't carry yourself like an adult in a business conversation (and by that I mean speaking clearly, asking the right questions, and being grateful and responsible), there won't be many people who will want to work with you.

Knowing these basic contract rules and legal responsibilities as well as having professional communication skills will separate you from the crowd and make you a business force of nature, a person brands want to work with again and again, versus someone who is only talented but lacking the ability to conduct business.

Build a Timeline.

Yes, there is such a thing as accidental success, but most successful businesses have been carefully planned with a timeline attached to their trajectory. Where do you want to be in three to six months? How about one to three years? What are your traffic goals for that time frame? How about revenue goals?

These are the reasons why a timeline matters:

- **It puts things in the right perspective.** No success is overnight, so if you create realistic goals and stick to them, you will eliminate some pressure of feeling like a failure if your success isn't instantaneous. Instead of telling yourself, "I want to be at a point X already!" you will have a very good idea about when you will arrive at that point based on your projections.

- **It motivates you.** There is nothing like a deadline to make you work more efficiently, even if you created it yourself. Sticking to your goals and timeline will bring a sense of organization to your work, and it will teach you to look at your blog as a business.

- **It makes things look more attainable.** A timeline divides your larger goals into smaller milestones and time periods and will make that bigger goal look more attainable. For example, if your current traffic is 10,000 visitors a month and you decide to do X, Y and Z to increase it 25% every month (which is completely doable), you will arrive at more than 100,000 visitors within one year. If I would have simply asked you how to get from 10,000 visitors to 100,000 and how long it will take without creating those incremental steps, you wouldn't have been able to answer with any certainty unless you had a plan and a timeline.

Building a timeline is essential for anything you want to accomplish, not just your blog. The only reason I managed to write this book in five short months while actively working on my business is the detailed timeline I'd built. At first, it sounded like an unrealistic project, but once I broke it down, I could see it coming to reality. I found out that an average novel contains about 40,000-50,000 words, and I had about 22 weekends to write. I realized that all I needed was to write an average of 2,000 words per week in order to finish my book in less than five months. Considering I write one or two blog posts every day, that number sounded completely achievable. The timeline made me disciplined about my writing. It's the reason you are reading this book right now.

The same strategy can be applied to your revenue planning. Try to answer a simple question: "How long will it take me to generate X revenue from my blog and make a living?" Make yourself accountable for your own timeline and schedule evaluation points for yourself. If you can't make money from your blog within one year, will you continue on the path you have chosen or change your strategy? Can you afford to continue dedicating ten hours a week to something that hasn't been generating any revenue? Is it possible to reevaluate and switch direction? All these questions are important if blogging is your business. Make yourself accountable for your own time and effort.

Make a Budget.

I'm a big believer in making an investment in order to see returns. Money doesn't grow just anywhere—you have to plant it at the right place and the right time, patiently watch it grow, then use some of the fruits to plant new seeds.

Luckily, in the case of blogging, you don't need much money to succeed. Most blogging platforms are free, and the only thing you will be investing in most cases is your own time (which *is* an investment, by the way).

Still, there are small, yet smart, investments you can make that will give you a competitive edge, and I'm surprised to see so many beginners passing on them like they were luxuries. So, here are the things worth the investment if you plan on making blogging your career:

- **Design and branding.** As I mentioned before, these things are extremely inexpensive these days. You can pay someone on *elance.com* $50 to design a logo; you can buy an elegant and effective WordPress template for $69. These little design touches do wonders in setting your site apart from others and can be invaluable when it comes to branding and positioning yourself as a professional rather than a fly-by-night hobbyist.

- **Developer.** You might want to consult with a developer to customize your theme and make sure your SEO (Search Engine Optimization) is in check. It might end up being a one-time expense of a couple hundred dollars. Most people I know spend this money on dinners and drinks in one week—wouldn't it be smarter to invest in your dream?

- **A good camera.** Even if you are not taking photos for your blog on a daily basis, it could be a great tool for you to create original content for your blog. If you look around at some of the most successful blogs out there, they rely 50% or more on their own photography—be it events they cover, photos of people they see or themselves. I'm not suggesting you need to spend thousands of dollars on a camera, but in most cases, your average cheap digital camera just won't have professional quality visuals. There are plenty of entry-level professional-grade cameras that will give you just enough quality upgrade for less than $700. The truth is, in today's blogosphere, the standard is pretty high when it comes to photography, and if you want to be considered a professional blogger, you definitely need the professional equipment to get in there and compete at that level.

- **Photo/video editing skills.** It's not enough to have the equipment if you can't easily edit the content you produce. Most good videos are cut in the right places, and the best photos are cropped and color corrected in all the right ways. Today's tools, even those available for free download, are extremely easy to learn and there is no excuse not to know them. If you are willing to spend a few hours on learning pro tools like Photoshop and Premiere (or Final Cut Pro), you will help yourself considerably.

- **Educational workshops and classes.** I'm a true believer in constantly educating myself on subjects related to my industry. When I first decided to start blogging on fashion, I took a few courses at the Fashion Institute of Technology in New York City on styling, fashion forecasting, and even a class for fashion designers on business, manufacturing and production. I felt it was necessary for me to understand the industry better before I could provide a valid opinion on any subject. Most of these courses cost me between $150-400 (thanks to FIT's status as a state university), and they provided me with invaluable amounts of knowledge and resources. I would also suggest classes and workshops on writing, photography and on-camera acting (if you are planning on creating video content).

- **Networking and professional events.** These are important not only for your education and staying abreast of new developments in your industry, but for meeting the right people and creating connections you can later continue. Most panels and conferences will cost you anywhere from $10-100, and some will require travel. In this case, I suggest you decide which ones are most important every year and allocate a travel budget for it. Meeting people outside your own immediate environment will foster and expand your network, so look at it as a great investment. For me, attending New York Fashion Week was a crucial part of getting where I am right now. This was the first place I met the majority of my blogger connections, which allowed me eventually to build Style Coalition as a blogger network. The $100 paid to IMG for the press pass back in 2007 could have been the smartest business investment I've ever made.

As you can see, most of these investments don't require a ton of money and you can expense most of them as they are professional investments in your own career. Considering most careers will require thousands of dollars to begin with, fashion blogging might be one of the more inexpensive choices.

By making a conscious decision to invest in your blog and your blogging career, you're committing to your success and making yourself accountable for making it happen.

Blogger Inspiration: Q&A with Kat Griffin of Corporette.

How did you come up with the name and the focus for your blog? Was it natural or did you have to limit yourself to a certain type, style, or niche?

I started my blog because I wasn't seeing the kind of fashion and lifestyle advice that I wanted for my own life, so the focus of the blog came totally naturally. Corporette is a fashion and lifestyle blog for women lawyers, bankers, MBAs, consultants and other "overachieving chicks" as we like to say. The name took me forever, though. I wanted my own domain name, and all of the good ones were taken! I think the final list of possibilities were Corporette, CEOChic, The Corporate Chick, Pink Pinstripe, The Pink Briefcase, and Honeybzz (I think I was going for a "worker bee" theme there). I even hired a designer to do a logo for CEOChic, but everything he did had a rather low-end feel to it. I finally went with Corporette just because I wanted to pull the trigger on something, but I wish I'd thought about how it sounds aurally. The first time I had a speaking engagement for the blog, which was emceeing a fashion show at a mall, the announcer kept saying, "And Kathy Griffin from corporate is here!" Sigh.

How did you build your audience? When was the moment you realized you have quite a large group of people reading your thoughts on a daily basis?

I built my audience by dumb luck. I was anonymous for the first two years I wrote it, so I couldn't even really promote it to my extended friends. I think I sent an email to about forty fairly close peeps saying, "Hey, check out this blog that my friend just started, it's awesome." It started to grow by word of mouth. After a few weeks of blogging, I posted an article about "Ten Things You Should Know About a Business Lunch"—basic etiquette that I'd seen a million junior associates screw up.

(Did I mention that I was a sixth-year litigator at a Wall Street law firm when I started the blog?) That post got picked up by the legal blog, "Above the Law," and my traffic *spiked*. It was so exciting! One of the biggest spikes in traffic I received at the time was in May 2009. There was some Bar event in Chicago where a panel of federal judges were speaking and the conversation wandered off topic into how some lawyers dressed really poorly for court. One of the judges mentioned my blog as a good resource, and then the whole conversation the judges had was picked up by national media—the *New York Times*, the *National Law Journal, Law.com*—even some local ABC outlets and things—all with links to my blog. As luck would have it this was exactly a week before my wedding and I already wasn't sleeping, so I was ill-equipped to handle the traffic. My hosting company shut me down after 30,000 hits and the email from the *Times* reporter asking for comment went to my spam folder, meaning I didn't see it until about two weeks later. Disaster!

Regarding the large readership base, I had worked as a magazine writer and editor before law school with my longest stint being at *Family Circle* magazine, which had a circulation of about 4.5 million at the time. Compared to that, my current readership (about 57,000 uniques each month) is small. But even in the beginning, when it was just 300 people, I was thrilled—there's immediacy and a connection with blogging that just isn't there in print. With a magazine, you write something, six months later it goes to print, and you never hear a word about it again— it's kind of like sending things into a void. With blogging, you can immediately see who's reading your stuff and where they're coming from.

What is your most popular blog post up to date? What made it such a viral success?

It would probably have to be "The Intern with the $9,000 Handbag," about a reader who wrote in to say she was just starting her law internship in Singapore and wondered if she should carry her Birkin handbag. I advised her "no" for a variety of reasons, and then 300+ commenters weighed in. *The Huffington Post* picked up the story, as well as a few other blogs, and it was a great success.

When was the moment you realized your blog was/is more than just a hobby? What made you believe it could be a full-time career?

I've always looked at Corporette as building a brand and a business. The numbers (traffic and money) keep climbing every month and that always gives me encouragement to keep going forward.

Did you quit your job or other occupation to make more room for blogging? Describe that process.

I just quit my job! It was a long process; I was a lawyer in a niche area of law that is very hard to get into in the first place (First Amendment media law), so I was reluctant to leave it. When I left my law firm in 2009, I went to a media-related non-profit and took a huge pay cut in part because I wanted more reliable, flexible hours so I could grow the blog. I finally was pushed over the edge because there was an article on a big business website about the top professional sites for women. They were nice enough to name me first as the "go-to resource," but from that article I studied my competitors, some of whom were already doing it full time. I decided that I still had a significant edge and a better focus than most of them and that I needed to invest what time and energy I could to keep and grow that lead in market share and notoriety.

What are some of the revenue channels for your blog? Which do you find most profitable and why?

Last year was the first time I did percentages: For 2010, it was 54% affiliate relationships, 23% ads, 9% speaking, and 14% direct partnerships with brands. My ad revenue is growing since I've hooked up with an ad network (Style Coalition), but affiliate revenue is still my primary source of income with the brand. This makes sense to me: the bulk of my readers are working at demanding, busy jobs, so not only do they not have time to hit the shops regularly, it may even be a struggle for them to get to the brick and mortar stores when they're open. A lot of their Internet shopping is done through Corporette, which is always a huge honor.

Name some of the brands and campaigns or collaborations you worked on as a blogger. How did these opportunities come about and what made these partnerships successful?

The biggest to date was a partnership with *InStyle* magazine and AK Anne Klein—they came to me when I was still anonymous and asked me to help promote some stuff. In the beginning, it was just going to be a banner ad and one speaking engagement (emceeing a fashion show at a Macy's) but it turned into four speaking engagements across the country. This was the first time I'd ever done anything like that, and it was thrilling, but it was also a great learning experience about the basics: how to hold the microphone, keeping my energy up, engaging the people who came to the event, and even how to interact with the marketing people from AK Anne Klein who came to the events. One of the other big partnerships that was so exciting was my first video shoot with Style Coalition, a shoot for American Living by JCPenney. The dress I chose and "modeled" was lovely, but I was really psyched to meet the American Living team, to work with a real videographer, and to start building my "reel."

What kind of opportunities have opened up for you as a full time blogger that you could not have done before?

Let's just say I'm still exploring those opportunities and weighing which ones work for me and my audience. Some of the hottest perks of blogging—the dinners, the fashion shows, the free gifts—aren't necessarily things my readers care to hear about, which means I have to weigh whether they're worth my time and energy.

What has been the highlight of your experience as a professional blogger so far?

It's tough to pinpoint one thing. Every day I feel so honored that Corporette has grown to be the success it is.

Is there one piece of advice you can give to aspiring professional bloggers?

Treat it like a business from the very beginning—have an editorial schedule and stick to it (but never apologize to readers if you miss it, because no one really notices!). Also, be wary of how you work with brands—make sure that the partnership is right for your readers.

What about one good warning for aspiring professional bloggers?

People can be fantastically cruel to you when they're anonymous and you're not. Every time I think I've grown a really tough skin, something else happens and I'm in a lousy mood for days. It's a huge learning process.

Is there anything you wish you could have done differently?

Not really. I've since learned that the "big money" is in the newsletters, and I sometimes wish that I had done Corporette as a newsletter instead. But one of the best things about the site is the community of women who comment daily, and that probably wouldn't have grown were it a newsletter.

What is one big dream you have as a blogger that you haven't realized yet?

I have a zillion plans for books—one for the bookstores, three for eBooks, and then a variety of other products. Beyond that, I see a lot of avenues for growing the brand and am just now getting the time to focus on them.

Action Items.

- Get a piece of paper and a pen and try to define yourself in a few key words. Focus on a few that might be relevant for your blog.

- Analyze your own resume to identify competitive advantages and areas of unique knowledge.

- Write your mission statement. First as an individual, then second as a blogger. Compare the two and make sure your personal goals are aligned with your professional ones.

- Create a business plan for your blog.

- Decide on a startup budget—including design help, equipment, workshops and industry conferences.

- Build a timeline for your success.

Chapter 2: Content

This is the part where you take all the ideas you've shaped in the planning chapter and start turning them into reality. The content of your virtual place (your blog) is a direct projection of who you are as a person. Think carefully about how you want to be portrayed and what kind of mark you want to leave behind with your content. Feel a sense of responsibility for this virtual space you are creating and the ways it may affect people.

This chapter will guide you to define the value you bring to other people and the ways you can translate this value proposition through the content you will create.

Content is also the main magnet for attracting your readers. I believe strong, original content is the only marketing technique you need as a blogger. This is what keeps readers coming back to your site every day and wanting to share it with their friends, creating exponential traffic growth for your blog. The power bloggers featured in the last sections of each chapter all agree and prove this theory.

This is the reason there is no "How to Get More Traffic for Your Blog" chapter in this book. There is, however, lots of advice on how to find your way to great content.

Define and Own Your Niche.

This is one of the most important decisions you will make when you start your blog. This will define who you are as a blogger, who you work with, and your revenue potential. Based on the first chapter, you have a firm grasp on what interests you most and what content aligns most closely with your personal goals and career path. Now it's time to focus on how this will affect your content.

These days, with the content overload on the Internet, it's more important than ever for a blogger to create a niche of consistent, strong content in order to keep readers coming back. Some key things to remember are:

- **Say it out loud.** Your blog focus should be "screaming" from your name, logo, design, every single post, mission statement page and your own profile. Make sure it's clearly communicated.

- **Keep it consistent.** Make sure all your other social media channels—Facebook, Twitter, and others—are in line with that niche as well. Of course you can post personal updates, but if you have a budget fashion blog and you keep talking about how much you love luxury brands on Twitter, you won't sound authentic.

- **Don't allow PR pitches to dictate your content.** If you are just starting as a blogger, you probably get excited every time you get an email from a brand representative or a publicist. If you have a decent-sized blog, you probably receive 10-100 pitches from public relations firms and in-house agencies on a daily basis. Some of them may contain great content, just not for your blog. It's a big dilemma, especially if you are just trying to establish your connections in the PR world. Your tendency will be to please the person behind the brand with a hope for future work together or perhaps other perks. Learn to decline politely and explain why the pitch doesn't fit your blog's focus. Most PR people will appreciate your integrity and professionalism. Tell them what YOU would like to feature and you will see how their pitches might change and eventually be useful to you.

- **Don't get distracted.** It's easy to get distracted by fashion news and major industry events. Sometimes big news happens and everyone keeps talking about a certain celebrity or a designer. You might feel like you want to be part of the discussion or at least provide your opinion. Use Twitter or Facebook to weigh in, but don't clutter your blog with non-relevant content. You will confuse your readers and might eventually lose some of them who aren't interested in other subjects besides your main focus. Your mission is not to cover everything in the fashion world, but provide value to your readers and stay focused on the subject of your blog.

- **Establish yourself as an expert.** Let's face it; in the online world, anyone can claim they are an expert. So, why not you? It's not only important to say it, but to back it up by demonstrating the necessary skills, constantly educating yourself, gaining accreditation, and being mentioned by other outlets (especially traditional press) either in quotes, commentary, interview, or a profile.

Offer yourself to reporters as a source of information, or make sure they find you via search. For example, my business blog gets lots of searches on the subjects of fashion and social media and innovations at Fashion Weeks. Some of these searches that lead people to my blog are coming from reporters who are searching for experts in this field.

One of these searches even resulted in a *Business Week* quote for me. The reporter searched for articles on the future of Fashion Weeks and runway shows in general, and I happened to write a blog post on the subject. After reading the post, the reporter found my email address on my blog's contact page and asked for a phone interview. Needless to say, a quote in *Business Week* was valuable for my credibility as an expert. I have many examples where my content drove in amazing press opportunities. In fact, most of my quotes in mainstream media were generated this way.

By clearly defining your niche, you make it easy not only for reporters and press to find you, but for people to describe and introduce you: "Meet Jane, she is *the* expert on plus sized fashion and writes a successful blog on the subject." See? Clear and simple. Want to make it even better? Find a smaller niche. Then you will hear something like this: "Meet Jane, she has an 80's-inspired blog on plus-sized fashion—it's my favorite daily dose of funk!" By doing something niche and unique, you not only inspire fans, but they become your blog's ambassadors, who market it to their friends.

Find Your Personal Voice.

Do words like *"feminine shapes," "edgy looks," "flowing fabrics," "interesting details,"* and *"designed for a confident woman"* sound familiar to you? You probably answered "yes" if you are a frequent reader of fashion blogs. We all are guilty of using and re-using the same language with the hope of sounding like an expert or perhaps with the hope of satisfying the people on the other side—designers and their PR and marketing people. This is how we believe the proper fashion review sounds, according to *Style.com*—our "Bible." The truth is, they all sound the same. Granted, some are more creative with words than others, while others sound like a thesaurus, but most are empty, non-impactful words. Isn't it strange that even when we have an almost unlimited amount of words at our disposal and the freedom to say what we want, we all choose to say the same thing?

Let's talk about your content originality as a writer and editor before we go any further. In today's blogosphere, the same content is published, republished, stolen, re-blogged, then stolen and republished again tomorrow, just in case the readers didn't catch the original. It's almost not relevant if the subject was seen first-hand, blogged about from photos, from a press release or, even worse, republished from a traditional news source.

As for the fashion news, we all know that *Women's Wear Daily* usually gets exclusives on the most newsworthy items and publishes them. Then the blogosphere chews them for the next few days. As an example, let's take the 2010 announcement of Julia Roberts signing as the new face of Lancôme cosmetics. Google indexed about 4,864 (!) blog posts after *WWD* broke the news on December 4th, 2010. Upon further inspection, a typical blog post that "broke" the story included a nice picture of the actress, one sentence describing the news and another paragraph quoted directly from the press release. Add an SEO-friendly title to top the story, and voilà! In under five minutes, they had created a new piece of content, the blog in question looked alive again and most likely that blogger felt like a real reporter, helping spread the news.

In reality, they just added to the clutter—the digital noise that continues to keep readers from connecting to real, effective content.

At the risk of sounding old and jaded, I will tell you that when I started covering New York Fashion Week, I was one of the first online to post reviews of the shows from my laptop sitting at the Bryant Park, sometimes no less than thirty minutes after the models left the runway. Back then, it was an effective way to build my name and audience. Today, this type of coverage disappears in the sea of blog posts, some based on the live-streaming video of the shows and written by people who are granted a virtual seat without the pain of the invitation process. And I promise they will have a better view sitting in front of their computers and zooming in on all the details. If not, there will be high-resolution photos from the show posted online shortly after. Based on these materials, anyone can write a story, or review, just like they were at the show.

So what's the point of running around this city in four-inch heels, dealing with the attitudes from PR and security, standing in lines— sometimes to be turned away because the show was overbooked—only to get a glimpse of five minutes of runway action behind people's backs for clothes that are not even relevant yet, because no one will be able to wear them until next season. What's the point?

Someone once gave me advice: *"Write what you saw and lived through,"* even if you saw it from behind other people's backs. I would add that the only thing that makes you different from others is your language and your point of view. Develop both with the same passion you develop your personal style, because they are a huge part of it.

Try this exercise: Go to Kate's Paperie and buy the most expensive, beautiful sheet of textured paper. Write your next blog post on this piece of paper, choosing your words carefully, because you can only write it once. Now compare it to a post on the same subject written directly on your computer.

There is something about the easiness of creating digital content and publishing it online that removes any filtering, any critical look or thought process of any kind. You get caught up in the race of posting more, being first to publish the news on your own site, getting more traffic, more readers, more comments, more everything.

- Imagine you were billed by the kilobyte to post content. Would you pay to publish this content?

- Imagine this could be the last thing you published before you died. Would you still post it?

- When you republish a piece of news fifty other sites have already published, what goal does that achieve?

Either you seriously believe your readers don't read any other sources and rely on you to provide all their information (which I would doubt), or perhaps you tried it once and enjoyed some traffic love from Google and people who searched for the newsy subject, which left you wanting more. I don't blame you—in a world where your influence is measured in large part by your traffic, it's hard to resist posting a hot piece of content the public is desperately searching for.

Try to forget the traffic numbers and think whether you are really adding value in a sustainable manner that goes back to your original mission statement and concept for your blog.

Mike Arrington of *TechCrunch* (one of the largest tech blogs out there) compares the collective noise and content clutter of the Internet to fast food. I compare it to fast fashion. A fast fashion company's philosophy asks: why would we waste efforts creating our own designs and perfecting the cuts if we could just copy someone else's work for much cheaper? Fast fashion already rules the retail market these days, the same way fast content rules the blogging world. A majority of the million blogs out there republish the same content over and over, with very little to zero originality.

The question is whether you are contributing to the clutter or adding value. Is your blog part of the "fast content" chain or do you prefer to have your own quality boutique and continue to create masterpieces no matter how little foot traffic your "proverbial shop" gets? This is the decision every blogger has to make.

Consider your blog or the content you put out there as a reflection of your true self. Would you still want to post the same things everyone else is posting? Is that really who you are? Do you desire to add to the clutter or actually bring some value to this world? What if, instead of requesting disclosures, the Federal Trade Commission requested you to disclose your reasons for posting each piece? What would be yours? Traffic, money, SEO, self-importance, bragging, attention, jealousy, judgment, boredom—or perhaps a true passion for the subject, the love for beautiful things, the desire to help, educate, share knowledge, encourage others, a craving for honest discussion with others, opening up your heart, saying simply what you feel and finding your own voice?

Years ago, people fought and died over freedom of speech, one of the main reasons for the founding of this country. We take this liberty for granted quite often in the US, but such free speech is still forbidden in other countries. Don't continue to take this freedom for granted. You are gifted the option to express your thoughts to the world, so speak from your heart; talk about subjects that matter the most to you. If you're truly passionate about fabrics, colors, and shapes, write about these things from your heart. If those colors make someone's life happier, you've accomplished your mission to bring value to this world and carved a niche for your content simultaneously. Everybody wins.

Develop Your Writing Style.

Once you've established the idea of what you want to write about, think about how you will communicate it. The language and words you use are a huge part of your brand and while it's hard to come up with rules for a "blogging language," if you want to build a business based on your content, you have to be aware of the rules and make conscious choices. Decide what language best reflects the principles of your brand and stick to it.

Beware of using profanity and common slang. Although things like cursing and slang can contribute to your colorful voice and resonate with certain readers, they can become a turn off when you wish to work with certain brands in a spokesperson capacity. Brands don't always like to take risks, and the majority of them have strict rules and guidelines when it comes to where they will lend their voice. Even if you know that you can turn this language on and off, depending on the subject, that's not blatantly obvious to other people and it could lose you some opportunities.

Beware of using language that is too intellectual or above the heads of your readers. Considering the low attention span in our digital age, make sure you write in a language your readers can easily understand. Using fancy words and narrow industry terms can be seen as elitist and disconnect you from your audience. There is a fine line between sounding authoritative and confident and using language and terminology that is patronizing and highbrow. Think what type of a reader you would like to attract, and use the language accordingly.

While the language that you use to communicate with your audience is ultimately your decision as a writer and creator, my suggestion would be to take a balanced approach. Showing diversity is a good strategy, which may position you well on the business side. Just like actors who play varied roles as part of their careers, you may do the same as a blogger, as long as you don't lose your own voice and authenticity. If you chose a friendly, casual tone, make sure to share some of your professional voice once in a while to remind readers it's there.

Just like shopping for your signature look, try on a few different writing styles before you settle on the one that suits you. See what resonates most with your readers. Watch their engagement levels and use your findings to craft future posts. Your writing style should evolve as your blog does—a natural process.

Your unusual language may become part of your signature, which is a great accomplishment, considering it's in line with your goals and compliments your brand. For example, in my fashion blog, *My It Things*, I try to infuse the word "It" in every post, making it fun and, at the same time, very recognizable. When I started, people would ask me twice for the name of the site, as it didn't make sense to some of them. I noticed today how many fashion sites are playing with this word in different expressions: "It" Girl, "It" Look, "It" Dress. I don't know if you could fully credit *My It Things* for the "It" popularity, but it's now part of the industry jargon.

Establish Confidence.

Confidence is an integral part of writing from the heart and establishing your own voice, as we discussed earlier. This is what separates you from the crowd of amateurs and positions you as a real professional. There is nothing wrong with raising questions and creating conversation at times, but the general voice of your blog must be confident if you wish to create a strong following and blog professionally.

There are a few reasons why your readers will be attracted to a confident writer rather than someone who plays with words:

- **People are naturally trained to listen to an authoritative voice.** By writing with confidence, you can establish yourself as an authority and make people listen. It almost doesn't matter if you are right or wrong, as long as you can confidently defend your point of view.

- **People like to get advice from confident people.** Just like you expect your doctor to be confident when you ask for medical advice, readers of your blog who seek style advice need to feel assured that you know what you are talking about. You can do it by adding credits and certificates to your résumé, getting quoted in the press, or doing TV appearances—all of which are extremely helpful in building the vision of yourself as an expert. However, if your writing does not exude confidence, all those credits become meaningless because you won't create an impression of yourself as an expert.

- **People like to be inspired and motivated.** Even though there are many ways to do so, confident and passionate writing is one of the best ways to convince people of your point of view. Make it your goal to inspire and motivate people on a daily basis, and don't be afraid to make bold statements even if not everyone can relate to them.

- **Confidence is one of the main qualities brands and advertisers look for in bloggers.** Companies want to work with professionals who have established confidence, expertise, and proven results. They look for bloggers who can project confidence into campaigns, which translates into sales, thus benefiting their product and justifying their advertising dollars. If you desire to become a spokesperson for a brand some day, your confidence is the ultimate stamp that will inevitably seal your position as an authority who can convince others to purchase the product you endorse.

- **Projecting fearlessness drives away negative comments and disagreements.** There is nothing more fruitless than arguing or trying to defend your position to a person who exudes confidence without fear. If you are such a fearless individual, this is your resistance practice. The more you perfect it, the less resistance to your ideas you will find. Establish the confidence within your voice as a blogger early on and save yourself jealousy and negative comments later when you are at the top and everyone is trying to take you down.

Confidence is an essential part of everything you do in your life, no matter what your occupation. As a blogger putting your thoughts out there on a daily basis, your confidence (or lack of it) will eventually show through the words and images you produce. This rule applies even more if you create videos with your image projecting every fear and insecurity you would never verbalize.

So be aware of any lack in your fortitude and **develop your confidence, just as if it was a muscle in your body that needed a daily workout.**

Blogger Inspiration: Q&A with Gala Darling.

How did you come up with the name and the focus for your blog? Was it natural or did you have to limit yourself to a certain type, style or niche?

Well, since Gala Darling is my name, I decided to use that as my brand. At the time I registered *GalaDarling.com* having your name as your URL was kind of the style! It then made sense to have everything under my name: my Tumblr, Twitter username, Flickr profile, and other accounts are all under my brand name, which keeps things simple. As for the focus of the site, I view my blog as a magazine, and I write for a certain type of woman on a variety of topics as opposed to sticking to one or two subjects. This way, I don't get bored, and I have free reign to write about whatever pleases me!

How did you build your audience? When was the moment you realized you had quite a large group of people reading your thoughts on a daily basis?

I've been writing online since 1996 and have wonderfully managed to retain that audience through my various personal and creative incarnations! But the key for me has always been in writing content that is useful and timeless. As for being aware of the size of my audience, I forget all the time how many people actually read my site, but it's always exciting when I'm reminded. I am always surprised when my readers approach me on the street!

What is your most popular blog post to date? What made it such?

Right now, it's a list of thirty-three movies to watch when you've got the blues! It's my most popular ever and I just wrote it recently! I'm always shocked by what goes viral. But as I've said, it comes down to creating content that people can actually use.

When was the moment you realized your blog was more than just a hobby? What made you believe it could be a full time career? Did you quit your job or other occupation to make more room for blogging? Describe that process.

I started my blog with the intention of it being a business. I had quit my job in New Zealand, moved to Australia, and I really didn't want to work in a shop or an office ever again. Blogging made the most sense to me and I really went into it with teeth gritted. Failure was not an option! Thankfully, my gamble has paid off!

What are some of the revenue channels for your blog? Without revealing details, which of them do you find most profitable and why?

I sell advertising, podcasts and digital products as well as holding online workshops and brand collaborations. They are all equally profitable, but only when I focus my attention on them. They all require a little work; none of them are really "passive streams of income."

Name some of the brands and campaigns or collaborations you have worked on as a blogger. How did these opportunities come about and what made these partnerships successful?

I have worked with Coach, Juicy Couture, Estee Lauder, Betsey Johnson, Google, Microsoft, JCPenney, Mary-Kate & Ashley Olsen, Samsung and many, many others. I'm either approached by the company directly or by someone who does PR for them. What makes a partnership successful is mutual excitement! If you're not feeling it 100%, the results will be subpar. You have to work with companies you believe in, and do something you enjoy.

What kind of opportunities opened up for you as a full-time blogger that you could not do before?

Pretty much every amazing experience I've had can be traced back to my role as a blogger... it's incredible! I walked in Betsey Johnson's show at New York Fashion Week this year, which was a total highlight of my life, since Betsey is my icon and a personal hero.

There are lots of little things, too. Some top bloggers are entitled to a lot of weird, cool perks. I was tweeting about a hotel in Miami the other day and two minutes later, the press rep for the hotel was emailing me, asking if I'd like a couple of complimentary nights and a press rate for the rest of my stay. All of those things make life much sweeter! It's important, though, not to get swept away and feel self-important. You have to remember you're only being awarded these perks because the company thinks they can get more out of you and your notoriety than you're getting out of them!

What has been the highlight of your experience as a professional blogger so far?

There have been lots of cool experiences—more than I could possibly cover. But at the risk of sounding cheesy, to me the best thing about being a blogger is that I'm able to do what I absolutely love every day. I love to write and share my ideas and discoveries, I love to communicate with large amounts of people, I love the Internet and I really love art and design. All of these things combined make for an extremely happy girl!

Is there one piece of advice you can give to aspiring professional bloggers?

I think it's like anything, really: in order to really be successful at it, you have to be insanely passionate. If blogging doesn't light you up like a pinball machine, then you shouldn't waste your time. Just because blogging is the hot thing right now doesn't make it right for you.

Is there a warning you can give to aspiring professional bloggers?

The best bloggers realize that the definition of elegance is making something extremely difficult look effortless. In other words: blogging isn't easy. It's not a get-rich-quick scheme! Expect to work your little booty off and then some!

Invest in Branding.

While the content itself is extremely important, if you are blogging as a business, it's the packaging that matters most. Your blog's name, domain, logo and design will be some of the most important decisions you will ever make as an online publisher. You will be identified with (and sometimes by) your blog name and branding for years. In some cases, it will become your second name, used more commonly than your real name at professional functions and within the industry in general. Think about it as your own powerful identity and choose wisely before committing to it.

Changing the name of your blog is a possibility later, but definitely not recommended and will require unnecessary effort and time waste. With that said, if your current blog name and identity aren't representing who you are anymore, or they stand in your way to becoming a professional blogger, there isn't a better time than now to consider new branding. Think well before choosing your new brand, change it quickly, don't apologize and never look back. Your loyal readers will stick with you, and new branding might invigorate loyal followers, attract new readers and bring new revenue opportunities.

A few things to keep in mind when choosing your blog's branding and identity:

- **Brand consistency.** Think how well it resonates with your chosen niche, with who you are as a person and with your writing style.

- **Your target audience**. Think about the audience you are writing for and how your brand speaks to them. Is it clear from just reading your URL what your brand is all about?

- **Your target sponsors.** What kind of advertisers and sponsors will your brand attract? Will the name of your blog limit your potential to work with certain brands? Do you accept this? For example, if your name contains the word "budget," chances are you won't be getting inquiries from luxury brands. That's fine, as long as you are willing to constrain yourself to predominately budget-friendly, mass-market brands. It still leaves plenty of opportunities for you, but you should be aware of this decision and be comfortable with the outcome when it comes to the expansion of your brand and profitability model.

Beyond the name of your blog, the second most important thing about your branding is the **design of your blog**. Elements such as your logo, header, theme and layout are extremely important for that crucial first impression you are trying to make in the fashion space. I'm always surprised how much some of my favorite beauty and fashion bloggers invest in perfecting their actual faces with most innovative skincare products and latest makeup and how little time or money they spend making their virtual face as attractive. This can make or break your online property and profitability. You both deserve to look your best, so invest in your blog as you would yourself.

Consider these few important things you can do today to improve your blog's appearance, from easiest to most complex:

- **Get rid of the clutter.** Look at your sidebar, as it's usually the most cluttered space on a blog. I'm sure you can find countless badges, links, promos and expired information there. Treat your sidebar as if it was costing you money to place things on it because it actually does. The sidebar is prime real estate for advertising, something you should keep in mind every time you agree to place someone's widget or promo on your sidebar for free (you shouldn't, by the way). Same goes for any affiliations and links to other sites. Think about how they serve you on your way to becoming a professional blogger, and most importantly, what value they add to your readers.

- **Play with fonts and colors.** You need basic Cascading Style Sheet (CSS) knowledge to do so (depending on your template), but once you get the concept, go ahead and try color and font variations to find the best version. While these might sound like a simple matter of taste, you will be surprised how much online readers are driven by the ease via which they can read text and absorb color when choosing their regular content destinations. For example, it's a known fact that most people have difficulty reading white text on a dark background. Same goes for fonts that imitate handwriting. Perhaps your background is too busy and distracts from the main content or your font is too small for most people with small notebook screens to read. Maybe the text color is lacking contrast from the background. All these little things can be easily tweaked and may significantly affect your traffic and the amount of time people spend on your site. Try to change one at a time and watch the changes in your traffic over a period of time. (A week is usually a good measure.)

- **Refresh your logo.** Even if you absolutely love your logo, do a simple test and ask your friends if they think it could use a little polish. Perhaps you've never invested in a professionally-made logo. The good news is that logos are extremely cheap and fast to produce these days. Try one of the crowd sourcing sites recommended in the Helpful Resources guide at the end of this book, or ask a designer friend for a birthday gift. It will be more than worth it to have a professional logo that speaks volumes to your brand and will repay you in dividends.

- **Reevaluate your template.** While it might sound scary, if you are using one of the big blogging platforms like WordPress (my personal recommendation), changing a template shouldn't take more than 30 minutes of your time. If you are serious about making blogging your career, invest in one of the premium templates that aren't used by millions of other sites and one that best serves your blog's branding and content needs. You can find amazing templates for just $50-70. Use the Helpful Resources Guide in this book or simply Google "premium WordPress templates." You will be surprised how many amazing ready-made themes are out there and how easy it is to change your entire online appearance in just a few moments.

This small investment of time can pay rich dividends over the life of your site, so please don't delay and make your blog look the best as soon as possible. It's a decision you won't regret.

Decide on Visuals.

When you blog about fashion, style, beauty or other visual subjects, the images you use play a big role in your blog's overall appearance. They are part of your brand and need to be thoroughly considered—like everything you put on your blog. Their quality is crucial to your success and determines whether you are taken seriously as a blogger or not.

While not everyone can be a great photographer, having a professional-grade camera and the ability to create beautiful, original visuals sets the standard pretty high in the blogosphere these days. Whether you like it or not, you are competing against thousands of extremely talented people equipped with the latest cameras and lots of free time on their hands to take beautiful, sometimes art gallery-quality shots. So take your visuals seriously and invest as much time in them as you would in your writing (if not more, in certain cases).

You have to decide on the subject of your visuals to keep your blog consistent. Do you focus on street fashion, celebrities, local events, product or your own style? Many recently successful blogs focus only on their own looks and photographs, which definitely helps in building your brand name and engaging a following. However, I think general fashion commentary isn't going out of style any time soon. You have to find out what works for you and focus on producing or finding high quality visuals on that subject.

If you decide to seek external sources of inspiration, here are a few ways to do so:

- **Image banks**. If you already are making some revenue from your blog and can consider a professional, high-resolution images license, it's truly one of the best choices you can make. If the initial money isn't there, consider a few free solutions that will allow you to post the same images as embedded widgets with some sort of advertising around them. Fotoglif is my personal free photo tool of choice. All you have to do is sign up for an account, and then embed the image bank photos on your blog—simple and free.

- **Creative Commons.** The Internet is full of free content you might be able to license for editorial purposes. Check out Creative Commons and read their licensing rules. Flickr is one of the sites that uses Creative Commons photos and places the attributes next to each photo so you can easily find out if the photo is available and under what conditions you may use it.

- **Photo exchange.** If you find a photographer or fellow content creator whose aesthetic you appreciate and would like to use in your posts once in a while, email them and ask permission to use their photos in return for credit and links back. In most cases, they will be happy to make a mutually beneficial arrangement. It's at least worth asking.

Creating your own imagery might be the hardest, but definitely the most rewarding, way to draw a passionate following. There is nothing that can separate you from the crowd better than your own, beautifully-created photos. Since we've talked about the importance of visuals on your blog already, make sure these are above-average quality. It's easy to create great photos when you have an expensive professional camera, so this advice would be mostly for bloggers who don't own one, but would like to create great looking photos:

- **Shoot in daylight.** Cheap cameras tend to make photos look ten times better in good lighting. Unfortunately, most nighttime photos will require a professional flash in order to get close to the desired quality. For best results, try to get most of your shots before the sun goes down. If shooting indoors, use a floor lamp or one of the clip-on lights to add additional source of light and brighten up your object.

- **Stage your photos.** Make sure the background is appropriate and not messy. Think about the way you would frame the photo and what kind of objects will make into that frame. Even in street style photos, everything needs to be thought through. Is there a garbage can behind your fashionable object detracting from the composition of the picture? Move it aside.

- **Keep it simple.** Since you don't have the ability to play with focus, everything will get the same amount of attention in your frame, so keep it simple. Focus the photo on the object and do your best to minimize distractions.

- **Enhance with editing software.** Here is where Photoshop (or similar image editing software) skills come in handy. If you are using a non-professional camera, you will most likely need to manipulate the lighting, contrast or colors of your photo to enhance the quality. You can get amazing results using the right tools, so it's worth experimenting if you don't want to invest in a professional camera (and sometimes even if you do).

It's important to keep the quality of your photos consistent; one bad photo can reduce the overall image of your blog. It can also lose some discerning readers; most people reading fashion and style blogs have a picky eye that won't tolerate low quality images.

Here again, as with your writing, it will benefit you greatly to continue to develop your skills and invest in workshops and classes that will help you get the most original, inspiring visuals.

Finally, remember that photography is not the only option for your visuals. Get your creative juices flowing and think about other options you can use to find visual materials. Maybe it's a Polyvore collage or scanning certain objects, or perhaps you have great artistic abilities and you could create your own illustrations for your posts. This will only add quality points and contribute to your overall originality and—even more so—become part of your brand.

Try to find that signature element that will set your visuals apart. Is there something that could be recognizable even if posted outside your blog? It can be a frame or a stamp added to every photo or some other recurring theme or idea.

When I started posting my outfit photos at the beginning of my blogging career, I took my own photos using a tripod and a remote control, taking the photos against the wall in my little office. It was boring just to stand there and pose, so I tried to jump in the air and press the remote at the same time. It created great movement in the photo and actually showed my clothes in a new, exciting way. I got more positive responses to these photos taken with a cheap pocket camera, than any professional looking photos I ever posted before.

Think about the conceptual part of your photos: what could possibly become your signature and set you apart from millions of other style blogs?

Enrich Your Content With Video.

You must have heard many times by now that online video is where the future is and might have even tried to play with your webcam or Flip camera creating some video content. If you have, then you've realized how challenging it is. The truth is, video content *is* the future, when done right. As a blogger, your video channel could serve a few great purposes:

- **Connect you with your audience in a deeper way**. Only video can show them who you really are, and they can feel more connected to you and your written content after getting a better sense of your personality on video.

- **Make your blog content come to life**. Yes, written word and photography have lots of power, but great video content can be ten times more powerful and illustrate your ideas in much more entertaining ways.

- **Expose you to a new audience via video distribution platforms**. People might find your blog via your YouTube channel and turn into regular readers.

- **Open additional revenue channels**. You can find brands that will be willing to sponsor your original video series or at least some of the episodes. Additionally, based on your video content, you could get hosting gigs or be invited to create branded video content. (More on this in the Revenue chapter.)

The main challenges to creating great video content are not only technical (great camera, editing software, sound recording), but also conceptual. The attention span of the average user on YouTube is mere seconds, which is all the time you have to catch their interest. Your content needs to be engaging, well-presented and in the case of fashion, visually appealing. This may seem to be a big task for an amateur video creator, yet we see quite a few bloggers successfully expanding their brand into the online video platform without much professional help. Here are some of the essentials you need to create sharp, engaging, memorable video content:

- **Keep it short.** Experts say a great online video is one minute long, and I agree. Most concepts can be conveyed in under one minute, but if you do need to expand, make it three to five minutes at the absolute longest. Put your best content in the first thirty seconds of your video.

- **Write a script.** The only way to fit everything you want to say in such a short period of time is to write a script. Even if you are trying to sound more casual and spontaneous, write a few bullet points to keep you on track.

- **Design your set.** Even if it's a home video, it doesn't mean you can't put some thought to your frame background—the colors and objects surrounding you. Keep it simple and clean up the space that will appear in the frame—you don't want unnecessary objects to distract the viewers. Pay attention to the colors of the walls and furniture and the way they coordinate with your outfit. Make sure the background colors aren't overshadowing you in the frame.

- **Look your absolute best.** I know it might sound obvious for someone who is into beauty and fashion, but I see so many bloggers look "too natural' in their videos. There are other ways to communicate your authenticity. If you want to position yourself as an expert, you have to look like one. There is a reason people on TV spend hours in hair and makeup before appearing on camera. The tricky thing about video is that it washes out your features if your makeup isn't applied properly. If wearing makeup, you'll need to go two shades darker in your eye and lip color for it to be noticeable on camera, and a great matte foundation is a key. So don't be afraid to go full on with your makeup.

Your clothes need to be neat and well-fitted (You've probably heard the saying that a camera adds ten pounds). I suggest bold colors for clothes, and staying away from small patterns and too much jewelry. Even though you're a fashion blogger, you'll want people to focus on your face and the words you are saying, not be distracted by your choice of wardrobe.

- **Turn up your energy**. One of the ways to keep the audience's attention with your video is to make sure it's dynamic, which is hard to do without great professional editing. So your only tool to keep your video alive is you.

  The secret only the pros know is simple: you have to be twice as animated and energized on camera. It might feel unnatural at first, but once you see the end result, you'll know that it just works. So find your inner energy switch and turn it up! I find that singing, jumping or dancing right before I record myself does the trick. You'll need to find out what works for you.

- **Annunciate and speak clearly.** There is nothing that loses an audience's attention faster than poor sound quality. If they can't understand what you are saying or there is a background noise in your video, people won't give you another chance and will close the video.

  If you don't have an external microphone, make sure you remain very close to the camera, shut the windows and eliminate all other sources of noise. Sometimes camera microphones can even pick up air conditioner noises you might not have noticed in your room. Do a sound test for 10 seconds to discover hidden noise distractions, then get rid of them before you shoot.

- **Be consistent with your content.** As with your writing, keep the content of the videos consistent. Once you've discovered what kind of video content you'd like to create, stick to it. Think what makes the most sense for your blog, what kind of video series would be a natural extension of your content, and what content translates best to video rather than a written post.

Make your video engaging by asking or answering readers' questions in your video and providing valuable advice. "How-to" videos tend to do really well online and will provide a great educational service beyond your blog. Think about the elements that will return in every video, the things that will make your readers come back and look forward to seeing on a regular basis.

- **Edit, edit, edit.** There is plenty of user-friendly online editing software that doesn't require any special skills. Even if you record your episode as one piece start-to-finish, there will be parts you could shorten or make a bit more dynamic while you talk. All you need to create your video segment is cut and paste different parts into your movie's timeline and export it as one piece at the end. Sometimes just a few minutes of editing will transform your video into a viral hit, and the advanced visual packaging will make it look more professional.

One of the most import factors to remember when creating video content is to think about it as an entertainment piece, which might be a different concept from your written content. Don't be afraid to add humor, sarcasm or even a simple smile. People want to be entertained, so make sure they are. Have fun with it and don't take yourself too seriously. After all, you aren't hosting a program on national TV. At least not yet!

Create Content Guidelines & Rules.

Being the sole owner of your business might make you assume you don't need guidelines or rules. After all, you can treat each case separately and decide how to proceed since it's your decision, right? Not really. The truth is, if you want to build a great basis for your business and be taken seriously, you must establish a set of guidelines, then follow them and clearly communicate them to others. This refers to content, comments, editorial policies, reviews, advertising—basically all the elements of your blog.

While some guidelines will be for your personal use, others should be displayed publicly. Why is it a good idea to clearly establish these guidelines for both for you and others?

- It projects a professional image.

- You become more disciplined in the ways you produce and format your content.

- You help your readers to adapt to certain elements and formats you use.

- You set expectations for readers, potential PR relationships and future sponsors.

- You make it easier for others to work with you.

- You save yourself unnecessary wasted time answering questions by creating a place to which you can refer people to view your guidelines.

- Your guidelines will help you make the right decisions if you are ever in doubt.

Here are some examples of personal guidelines that are best kept private:

- **Frequency of publishing content.** Are you posting once a day, three times a day or three times a week? Come up with a realistic schedule and stick to it. Even if you are able to post only once a week, but your posts are visually rich and thought provoking, it might be enough to keep the responses and conversation among your readers going for a whole week. Write strategically based on your content calendar and never apologize for not writing enough, or taking time off from writing. Just get back right to where you were, and keep producing great content.

- **Subjects to avoid.** If you decide not to publish celebrity content, stick to your decision, even when it's tempting. Your regular readers will appreciate your editorial integrity.

- **Regular themes and columns.** Do you have certain themes that repeat from week to week? Are they posted on a certain day of the week or in random order? It might be a good idea to create a few columns because they create a certain addiction and expectation among readers, especially when they are repeated on the same day of the week. For example, Gala Darling is known for her signature "Things I Love Thursday." I've been reading her blog for years and don't remember her missing even one Thursday with this column. Now that's dedication! Think about subjects you can commit to and make them your signature columns that people will look forward to every week.

Now for some examples of public guidelines and rules, best published on your blog in a prominent spot:

- **Commenting guidelines.** This will set expectations for your readers on what is and isn't allowed on your blog.

- **Editorial rules.** This will state the subjects and products you will and won't feature on your blog. This will help PR companies to pitch you most effectively and guide them on the most appropriate subjects with which to approach you.

- **Product gifting and reviews.** This is a controversial subject widely discussed in the blogosphere and recently regulated by the Federal Trade Commission. Beyond your legal responsibility to state when free product has been received, it might be a good idea to share some of your rules, such as what kind of products you will accept for review and the best procedure to inquire about product review on your blog.

  If your blog's content relies heavily on reviews, you should definitely have your rules spelled out to manage expectations both from readers and brands. While there isn't any other way to review beauty products other than to try them on, with fashion, things are different, and receiving a product as a gift definitely creates some conflicts.

  The best way I've found to prevent those conflicts is to never post a standalone personal review for a gifted fashion product. I'm more comfortable mentioning it in my stories or crediting it when I wear the piece, but raving about something you received as a gift might not sound authentic and turn away valuable readers.

- **Sponsorship guidelines.** Most blogs feature advertorial or sponsored content. State your position on the subject, rules you follow with respect to such content and the best way to inquire about placing these items on your blog. There will be more on advertorial content in the Revenue chapter.

Start by outlining the basics and keep these guidelines updated as you stumble upon new cases requiring you to establish new guidelines. It's a great way to set a strong basis for top blogging content, and it will keep you on track as more and more opportunities arise.

Understand the Difference between Editorial and Promotional Content.

The choice of subjects you feature—and more importantly, don't feature—on your blog might be one of the most important decisions you make as a blogger. Being selective defines your editorial integrity and your voice as an independent writer.

These days, bloggers are constantly being pitched content ideas on anything and everything—from news to magazine editorials to Facebook contests—all the way to pure advertising campaigns. The matter gets more complicated when the pitch is sent from one of your favorite brands. By featuring promotional content on your blog, you might not only lose readers, but also potential revenue.

To illustrate, I can share a recent example from my network, in which a big advertiser wanted to purchase a series of advertorial postings, one of them on blog X. After searching for the advertiser's name on that blog, they found that the blog already posted the same promotional content for which they were willing to pay. Obviously, we couldn't include that blogger in the paid campaign, which means they lost revenue, and possibly a potential future client for paid advertising.

Those decisions are especially hard as most fashion content is centered around shopping, and many blogs feature sales and special discount events as part of their regular content. There is nothing wrong with that, if that's part of the focus of your blog. However, this decision needs to be strategic, and you have to weigh all the cons and pros before featuring anything that might be too promotional. If you are going down this path, you might end up with a blog that looks like an online coupon book, rather than a source of knowledge and inspiration.

How do you learn to differentiate between content that is valuable to your readers and content that is hurting your authenticity? Here are a few questions to ask yourself:

- **Does it add value to your readers?** Will they be interested in actually reading about this subject, or will they feel like they're been duped into reading an advertisement? Avoid sounding like a commercial.

- **Does it have a story?** Some promotions can be pretty clever and have an interesting/unique story behind them. Focus on the story to engage the reader and enrich your content versus simply reiterating the promotion.

- **Was it advertised on other sites?** Have you seen this content as a paid banner, advertorial or newsletter campaign on other sites? Make sure you don't give for free what others are getting paid to produce.

Even though it's sometimes hard to make both business and editorial decisions as an independent publisher, you have to listen to your business voice at all times. Stick to the defined voice you've set for your site and to the set of rules you have created. Remain firm in your commitment to build your business.

Finally, don't let anyone convince you to change these principles, unless it makes sense to you as part of your progression. Maintaining a fine line between editorial content and paid advertising will not only strengthen your voice but also position your voice as one to be trusted—one that readers will return to again and again and reference for years to come.

Blogger Inspiration: Q&A with Lauren Dimet-Waters of Second City Style.

How did you come up with the name and the focus for your blog?

When my business partner Carol Calacci and I first came up with the idea for Second City Style in 2005, we looked at our site as an actual on-line fashion and beauty magazine. We had no idea what a blog was back then, so we didn't even add the blog component until ten months after our launch. We also thought our focus would be fashion and beauty in Chicago, IL, which was pretty short-sighted considering our site was on the web. We found out quickly we had followers outside of Chicago. We now cover everything. It's exhausting when you try to hit all points on fashion and beauty nationally. That's why we have multiple editors writing for us at any given time. It's too much for two people. I wish we had a more narrow focus, but it's too late.

To this day, we don't consider ourselves "bloggers" and cringe when that term is used. We are online publishers. We publish few magazine articles per week and update our blog section 6-10 times per weekday. Thankfully, we take the weekends off. Recently, we merged both the magazine and blog into one site.

How did you build your audience?

At first we were thrilled if we had 200 visits in a day. We did little to build our readership back then because we had no idea what we were doing. It wasn't until a year into publishing the blog we realized quite a few people read us. I remember being at a New York event four years ago and casually introducing myself to a woman when she freaked out! My husband was there to witness her telling me we were one of her absolute favorite daily must-reads. That was very gratifying.

What is your most popular blog post up to date?

One of our most popular posts to date is an investigative report I did right after I got married in 2007. There was a Chinese dress manufacturer that was not only ripping off well-known bridal designer's work, but was using their actual photos on their site! Shocked and dismayed, I alerted some of the affected designers who had no clue this was happening and even got them in touch with an attorney for a class action suit. Luckily, they were able to shut them down before a suit had to be filed.

When was the moment you realized your blog was/is more than just a hobby? Did you quit your job or other occupation to make more room for blogging?

I had been working in technology for several years and about the time we were putting Second City Style together I was in a hateful job for a spiteful company. I actually quit sooner than I should have, or was ready to, but I just couldn't take the abuse anymore. I figured if I would rather starve and work for myself than continue a job I hated! So my pet project was suddenly more than a hobby out of sheer necessity. I made this a full-time career by simply doing it full time.

What are some of the revenue channels for your blog?

We earn revenue several different ways. Ads like Ad Sense, Blog Ads and our Style Coalition ads bring in revenue. Also affiliate sales are fantastic if your readers actually buy. We work primarily with LinkShare, Commission Junction, Google and Pepperjam. There are a few smaller ones too. You need readers who shop in order to make money this way, so think about your audience when you put a look together. Will they buy it? If you cater to twenty-something hipsters, for instance, make sure what you pick are products they will really buy.

Our mailing list has proven itself to be quite useful for sending dedicated emails. We sell our dedicated email service directly. We can break our list into targeted geographical lists so advertisers can pinpoint an exact audience if they desire. Our Chicago list is quite popular as is our national one. We built our list through our monthly giveaways and the smaller giveaways we host on the blog. Readers may also sign up for our email list directly on our site. We send out newsletters ourselves periodically. Since our email list is so important to us, we don't like to send out too many notifications and annoy our valuable readers. People will ask to be removed. We do some dedicated posts, but it has to be a product we stand behind.

What kind of opportunities have opened up for you as a full time blogger that you could not have had before?

Some of the opportunities that have come our way because of blogging include getting invited to some really amazing events in NYC and Chicago as well as covering New York Fashion Week! I remember when we first launched, we could hardly get invited to an envelope opening. I would go and buy makeup to test for posts or write about the perfume I was wearing at the time. We never got samples to review at first, now we do.

How did we make it? When we first launched, we hooked up with The Chicago Fashion Resource, the City of Chicago's Fashion Week and GenArt Chicago. We then met Chicago fashion makers and designers. Once we started covering events, we received more and more invites. Then some of the department stores like Saks, Marshall Fields (now Macy's), Nordstrom and Neiman Marcus contacted us and eventually designer's PR companies in both Chicago and New York began reaching out. It all just snowballed from there. As for beauty product reviews, eventually covering my favorites from my own makeup bag paid off. Beauty PR firms began contacting me to see if I would like to try a sample of their new products. I remember doing a post on the "right red lipstick for your skin tone" a few months after we launched. It took me days to scour drugstores and department stores to put it together. I was sent a lot of red lipstick after that. Too bad I didn't get those before I started my research. Now if I have a story idea, I can email my PR contacts and see what they have that fits. Additionally, we added a beauty editor about six months after we launched who came up with the idea for our annual Beauty Olympics. We now get tons of products to test every fall. It's overwhelming now. In fact, we are now going to scale it back.

What has been the highlight of your experience as a professional blogger so far?

The highlight of my blogging career is meeting and having relationships with some of the designers I have admired for years. When they remember me, I get a thrill. They are my personal rock stars and celebrities.

Is there one piece of advice you can give to aspiring professional bloggers?

Some advice I can give to new bloggers, is if you are going to launch a blog today, have a niche. An angle that nobody else is doing. I know this is the advice most give, but there is a reason we keep repeating it. You have to be different these days to get noticed. There is a glut of blogs, so unless you have longevity, you need an angle. Otherwise, you will be swimming upstream and probably give up.

What is one big dream you have as a blogger that you haven't realized yet?

My big dream is collaborating on a maternity line or something similar. I need to develop a product line! I'm waiting for my *Bethenny Frankel* moment... or a TV show.

Action Items.

- Make a list of your favorite blogs and try to find out what makes their writing style appealing. Make a list of these elements and try to incorporate them into your own writing.

- Go to Kate's Paperie or your local fine paper retailer and buy the most expensive, beautiful sheet of textured paper. Write your next blog post on this piece of paper, choosing your words carefully, because you can only write this once. Now compare it to a post on the same subject written directly on your computer.

- Come up with a list of subjects you would like to be pitched about and send it to PR contacts you have.

- Email a reporter you respect and offer yourself as an expert any time they need a quote on the subject of your blog.

- Confidence exercise: go back to your blog posts and try to re-write a few without using the words "maybe", "not sure", and "In my modest opinion". Consider stronger words and phrases, such as "In my opinion," "I think" and "I believe."

- For one week, take your camera everywhere and use it as a second set of eyes. Ask strangers and friends to photograph you in different situations. Try to capture as many photos as you can. At the end of the week, look at all the photos and see what inspires you most, what could be incorporated into your blog's content. Some of the photos could even give you ideas for recurring columns, which may turn into your signature.

- Write a script for a video segment that relates to the subject of your blog. Set up a camera and tripod and get a few takes of you "hosting" the segment. Use different moods, characters and voice tones on camera. Watch them to find out which works best.

Chapter 3:

Relationships

The greatest thing about blogging is that it's a social activity—allowing you to engage, interact, connect and hopefully influence the masses. Readers, fellow bloggers, PR and marketing professionals are vital to your success, but always remember that behind all these titles are real people who have personalities, egos, characters, passions, insecurities, talents and feelings. Some will become your closest friends; some will teach you surprising lessons about yourself and the world. This chapter will guide you in crafting a network of valuable professional connections and effectively managing different kinds of relationships. It will show you how to create and forge powerful connections that will become invaluable along your path as a professional blogger and business person.

Connect with Your Readers.

This is where all of your relationships will begin, and it's the most important relationship you will ever have as a professional blogger. Although you write for yourself and your blog is an outlet of self-expression, without people caring about what you have to say, you will never be considered a top blogging professional. The amount of people listening to you is less unimportant. What's important is the level of their engagement with your content and the influence it has on their lives.

The first thing you'll want to do is learn more about who is reading your site. Get to know your readers by researching their profiles when they comment and by looking into your demographic stats on Google Analytics, or any other measurement platform you use. You can discover incredibly rich information—anything from the cities they live in to how often they read your blog. If you want to gain deeper knowledge, tools like Quantcast can tell you their gender, income level, even the number of children in their household. This is pretty valuable information which can (and should) affect your tone and content in order to build relationships with these people.

What are they going through, and how can you help them achieve what they are seeking from your words and images? Try to define early on what kind of relationships you want with your readers. Do you want many "passers-by," or would you rather develop a small group of dedicated followers that will religiously read every word you are saying? Are you interested in creating a conversation and hearing what your readers have to say, or simply sharing what you want to have them read? Do you want to be your readers' "best friend," or an expert they turn to for an advice? Answering these questions will color the tone of your voice and the way you present the content on your blog. They will also define the nature of your relationships with your readers.

Why is it important to define these relationships?

- **Reader relationships influence your personal brand.** If you are positioning yourself as an expert and your readers look to you for advice, you might be able to expand your brand and expertise into other channels, such as books and TV appearances. If your blog is more of a conversation with your readers, this may highlight your great social skills, which could be used in variety of other formats, such as hosting offline gatherings and events and teaching others to do the same.

- **Reader relationships also define your revenue channels.** In many cases, the level of your engagement with your readers will dictate the ways you are able to monetize your blog. For example, if company X is looking to create a conversational marketing campaign, they will most likely work with bloggers who have higher number of comments, versus those who have a larger number of visitors.

Think strategically: what types of relationships are appropriate for your blog, its niche, and most importantly, what suits you as a person? Even if you decide to completely disable the comments section on your blog (which some bloggers do these days), don't lose that connection to your readers. It should come through your writing tone, the subjects you choose and promotions you run. Always ask yourself, "who will be reading it and why?"

Socialize with Fellow Bloggers.

Being a blogger automatically makes you a member of the blogosphere. Although you may craft your content in a solitary state, you will advance your skills and business connections by socializing with other bloggers. This can be done online and offline in almost every city in the world. If that's not the case, create a goal to attend a big industry event like New York Fashion Week at least once a year to meet and connect with others who share your business and personal interests.

I've made most of my connections with fellow bloggers by attending New York Fashion Week and by creating my own networking group called Fashion 2.0 on *Meetup.com* back in 2008. This group was invaluable in helping me to advance my career and even in finding business opportunities. While I realize living in New York City makes it much easier to build your network, I've seen many bloggers have the same level of networking success through online mediums, especially Twitter and Facebook.

Whether you decide to join a blog network or connect with fellow bloggers individually, select those with whom you wish to network and make sure to connect with people you respect and can learn from professionally. Support their achievements; see them as assets that help your common goal—making the blogosphere a more professional and more profitable space.

Something you want to avoid at all cost is comparing yourself to other bloggers or asking yourself why some of them are more successful. **Make other bloggers your daily sources of inspiration, not your daily source of envy.**

Looking back to when I began blogging, I must admit I spent a lot of time (or more time than I should have) researching and analyzing my "competition," and sometimes feeling envious. Sometimes I couldn't explain why site X gets more traffic than my site, although my site had better quality content, prettier design and lots of fun contests. I would get envious of every big press feature my competitors would be mentioned at ("Why wasn't I quoted in this article?") And maybe the biggest of them all was "money envy." Every time someone in our space would close a big advertising campaign, seal a partnership or raise a round of financing, I would think X was better than me and ask myself why I failed to do the same.

At some point, through my personal development and a few unpleasant lessons along the way, I started realizing that those feelings of envy were hurting me and my ability to move forward. While being aware of your competition is definitely a must for everyone, **there is a fine line between being aware and being envious.** It took a while to analyze those feelings and deal with them so I could move on in my career without any baggage. I found those feelings of envy being dangerous for multiple reasons.

When you envy someone, you focus your energy on glorifying the other person and criticizing yourself. Let's break it down. Basically, you spend significant amount of time, energy and focus on thinking that competitor X rocks. By doing that, you are basically helping them to become even more successful and taking valuable time and resources away from making yourself the best you could possibly be. Wouldn't you want to direct this energy into your own projects instead? One of my greatest realizations when dealing with my own issues in the past was that when I envy someone I basically criticize myself at the same time. It literally means that I think person X is better/smarter/luckier than I am. Why would I direct such negative energy towards myself and my projects? The answer for many of us lies in our past, in some experience that made us feel less than accepted, less than the best. Deal with these issues ASAP, as they will only hurt more as both you and your business grow.

Envy distracts you from finding your successful path. Are you familiar with "could have/should have?" Yes, you could have been there before your competition and won the race, but what good does the regret do you now? Each one of us has chosen our own path, our own circumstances, and our own conditions. Envy causes you to look unnecessarily behind you at your past decisions rather than looking forward to the success awaiting you. You can't move swiftly forward if you're looking behind yourself.

So, next time you find yourself with the feelings of envy towards another blogger's press buzz, traffic, revenues or anything else you don't have that they appear to have, try to analyze if any of these points are important to *you*, then **set a plan on how to achieve them, instead of chasing someone else's success**.

Build your relationships with other bloggers based on the principles of partnership, as if you worked together for one big corporation called the Blogosphere, and each of you had an effect on how this company is perceived by others, how productive it is, how much its revenues are growing, and how positive the collective employee spirit may be. When you see yourself part of a bigger, your sense of self worth and eventually your actions can affect your bottom line. Positive relationships only help all of us grow in power and profitability, and there's more than enough wealth and prosperity to go around.

Connect with Public Relations Companies.

No matter the subject of your blog, your relationships with public relations companies are a big part of your success. They influence your content by providing you exclusive news and materials. They influence your income stream by introducing you to the brands you might have no direct connection with, and by inviting you to exclusive events and launches where, besides getting original content, you have the opportunity to create personal connections as well as network.

Those relationships should be managed carefully, as in most cases, you will be dealing with companies that represent multiple brands and one mistake can sour the overall connection and result in losing multiple connections.

Let's focus on how to make the initial connection:

- **Your content.** Keep in mind that everything you put out there will be seen, especially by the brands you are writing about. Most brands have a Google alert set up on their name or use other advanced coverage measurement techniques so that every time their name is mentioned somewhere online, they receive a notification, which they track and report. If you write about a specific brand, it's most likely the brand's PR and marketing people will see it. If the people behind the brand think your blog is the right outlet for their future news, they will eventually start reaching out to you and hopefully even supply exclusive content and stories. Think carefully about the kind of content you are putting out there and the brand names you are mentioning. The law of attraction works amazingly well online—you get more of what you put out there.

  I find writing about a brand to be the most effective way to attract the right brands to work with you. Write about them first and see if they reach out. Of course, you shouldn't write about them solely for this purpose, but if you are a big fan of the brand and see yourself working together in the future, make sure you incorporate them into your content.

My own relationship with Louis Vuitton started after I wrote a personal post about Catherine Deneuve featured in their "Art of Travel" campaign few years back. It truly evoked some nostalgic feelings in me, as I have been a big fan of the iconic actress (and French movies in general) since an early age. I wrote a personal post mentioning the campaign without any hidden agenda and was surprised when, just days later, I received a personal email from Louis Vuitton's head of PR. It was back in 2008, and I almost had to pinch myself while reading it. The email invited me to LV's first-ever intimate bloggers event, where we had a chance to meet the company's CEO for a private breakfast, and where I also met some of the top NYC fashion bloggers for the first time. It all started with one post.

- **Blind introduction.** This might be the hardest way to get a brand's attention, but if the fit is right, there is no reason it won't work. Find the appropriate contact through the brand's website or Google the internal PR contact or agency contact (most cases) for the brand. Come up with a concise 2-3 paragraph email describing your blog and its reach and an introduction about yourself. Tell them why you would like to get exclusive news and announcements from the brand and ask to get on their press list.

- **Introduction through your network.** This is where building connections with fellow bloggers comes in handy. When you feel comfortable, ask one of the bloggers who is already working with the brand for an email introduction. Yes, bloggers tend to be protective of their relationships with brands, but if you manage to create a true online friendship, not position yourself as a threat, most people will be open to helping you out. I get asked many times by brands about some other bloggers I would recommend them working with. I'm always happy to recommend one or two people who could be a good fit for the brand and who I respect professionally. Besides giving you "good karma" with other bloggers, the people behind the brand will appreciate your help in navigating in this crowded space.

- **Story pitches.** Rather than asking for a general introduction, come up with a specific story angle you would like to feature for this particular brand, or think how you can incorporate in your editorial calendar. When you have a well-thought through idea for an editorial feature, companies will be more willing to work with you. It will be easier for them to see how their brand will be incorporated into your content; therefore, they will feel more comfortable sharing materials and exclusive details with you.

   You could either come up with one specific story or a series of posts. For example, you could create a feature such as "Fashion Designers' Favorite Vacation Spots," which will run on a weekly or monthly basis. Then reach out to a PR company representing a particular designer and ask for a quick quote and recommendation. I can almost guarantee that if they enjoy your blog and the request is simple enough, they will do their best to provide you with the exclusive content. After all, that's their job!

In general, it would be great to approach your work with PR companies as a partnership, where you both are helping each other. You are helping them to reach their goals for their clients, and they are helping you to get the most interesting, original stories to keep your readers coming back every day. It's a win-win!

It is important to know what kind of agency you are dealing with so you can separate your editorial relationships from revenue generating opportunities. Note that many agencies are dipping into both worlds these days, so it's important to discern the differences between all types of relationships.

- **Traditional public relations agencies.** These are the people who are responsible solely for the press releases, samples management and press events for a particular brand. You may contact them for quotes, news, product images, product samples and event invites. Never ask these agencies for sponsorship or advertising opportunities. You will waste your time and look unprofessional by doing so. Examples of such agencies: *BPCM, Paul Wilmot, KCD, and People's Revolution.*

- **Social media agencies:** More and more brands are hiring these companies in addition to the traditional PR to help them navigate the complex online media landscape. Their duties might include management of brand's Facebook page and Twitter accounts, as well as assistance in building relationships with bloggers. Sometimes these agencies have promotional budgets and are willing to compensate bloggers for advertorial content or hire them for various promotions, such as hosting an event for a brand or filming an online video. These budgets are usually smaller than those managed by the marketing agency, because most of them work on a retainer basis just like PR companies. The retainer covers mostly internal agency costs and usually doesn't have much room for blogger fees and compensation. Agencies examples: *Attention, 360i, Big Fuel, and Ogilvy 360.*

- **Marketing and advertising agencies:** These companies manage the overall marketing budgets for brands, including display media (banners), print media, promotional events, sponsorships and the overall marketing strategy. While they would be the right people to build relationships for revenue purposes, they rarely work with blogs on an individual basis, unless you have millions of monthly visitors. Usually, the only way to get a slice of these budgets is through various advertising networks. Examples of such agencies: *Razorfish, Porter Novelly, Media Kitchen, and Morpheus Media.*

While these are the official definitions of the agencies roles, many of them overlap services. Some PR agencies have started providing social media services and more social media agencies are getting marketing budgets which could be used for larger, more complex promotions. Do your research on the agency before reaching out with any requests and especially before asking for money. We'll speak more on that later in the Revenue chapter.

Attend Industry Events.

Industry events are where most of your networking and relationship-building will happen. While online communication is great, nothing replaces in-person contact. If you live outside a major city like New York, connect to your local community to be on top of what's going on. When you do visit a major city on a vacation or other trip, make sure to schedule a few industry events into your trip.

How do you get invited? Once you establish online relationships with some of the agencies which represent the brands, ask them to get on the press list for invites to some of the events they put together. In most cases, you will be automatically added to their invite list once you are agency "approved," but it doesn't hurt to make sure you are actually on their list.

Alternatively, if you hear about a brand event, email and politely request a press invite. Explain who you are, what your blog is about and why you think it's important for you to attend. If you can't get on the list yourself, ask a friend who is attending to take you as their guest, if that's an option, and try to introduce yourself to the appropriate person during the event. Sometimes seeing and talking to you in-person can help the PR people to get a better sense of you professionally.

If you do get the opportunity to attend an industry event, it's always important to remember that your behavior will impact your ability to be invited to other such events. Remember, many industry events are high profile and often include celebrities, so creating situations where the publicist is unable to do their job making sure the guests and notables are comfortable will swiftly end your blogging career. Showcase your good manners and create a reputation of a guest everyone wants to have at their events. This includes moderating your intake of alcohol at the event, respecting the wishes of publicists when it comes to Tweeting and capturing photographs, and generally maintaining a well-mannered position when it comes to dealing with other guests. Save behavior best suited for nights out with your friends for party time. Industry events, even though they are often quite fabulous, are for business and networking, no matter how irresistible it might be to act out at times.

As a side note, if you do have a working relationship with a brand and you aren't invited to one of their events, don't make them uncomfortable by asking why unless you are 100% sure there was some sort of mistake. Brands have their own agendas regarding who, when and why they invite to events. Their press list is usually long and sometimes it's not an option to have everyone invited at the same time. Be respectful of their decision and try to never take it personally.

Over time, make an effort to create as many personal connections as you can without being too agenda-driven. I find that the relationships that turn the most valuable and profitable are created by having a sincere connection to a person rather than the company or brands they represent. It doesn't mean you have to become friends with every person you work with, but try to get to know the individual with whom you are speaking, their drives and objectives. Show them your personality and make a memorable impression. Help them to differentiate you from hundreds of other bloggers.

You can also use industry events to connect to your fellow bloggers. Find a few people you can trust and share with them some of your questions, concerns and doubts. When you work independently, it's great to have someone you can ask for an opinion once in a while, as well as from whom you can get some in-person inspiration and honest feedback.

Go to Fashion Week.

If industry events are great for building all sorts of connections, attending Fashion Week is the best way to do so on a tight schedule. Within one week, you can attend tons of events, find exclusive content, connect with lots of PR companies and brands and finally, meet countless people who can help you advance your blogging career.

Even if you live outside a major city hosting one of the fashion weeks, it's worth making a trip for a few days, as an investment in your career.

Now that you've decided to go, how do you actually get in? In this book, we will focus on New York Fashion Week specifically, but many of the rules and tips apply to international fashion weeks as well.

There are two main ways to get invites to the runway shows and presentations which are part of the official NYFW schedule: registering as a press member via the website or by asking individual designers for invites to their shows.

Registration is the best way to go but is more challenging because of the very selective approval process by the organizers. Every year, thousands of bloggers apply for press credentials, but only a small percentage gets in. It's still worth applying for, season after season, as the rules are bending more in favor of bloggers. Here are a few tips to remember for your application:

- **Apply early.** Make sure you apply as soon as registration opens, usually two months before the event itself. You will have less competition and will get the full attention of the person behind the approval process. You will also have more time to request reevaluation in case you get declined. More on that later.

- **Fill out the application carefully.** This is where your attention to detail is examined. Every question has a reason behind it, so even if it's optional, try to provide as much info about your blog, your credits and achievements. This is not the moment to be shy, but at the same time, not the moment to lie or overestimate your actual influence. Things like press features and TV appearances are worth mentioning, as well as any other coverage you've done for the designers showing. Provide links or screenshots to any of the above. Describe in a concise manner your blog's focus, its launch date, audience metrics, monthly unique visitors or page views and any affiliations that might help raise your profile, such as any blog network to which you belong. If you've attended and covered one of the fashion weeks already, make sure to include a link to your past coverage.

- **Do not take *no* for an answer.** This is good advice for anything you do in life, but is especially important in regards to attending Fashion Week. If it is very important for your blogging career, fight for a chance to be there. I myself was declined press credentials to NYFW in the past, simply picked up a phone and talked to the right person, explaining why I deserve to be there. Guess what? The "mistake" was fixed within moments, and I got my credentials. Sometimes the person on the other side needs the extra proof you are a professional and committed to your craft. Imagine yourself going through countless blogger applications and trying to decide who deserves credentials—it's a tough choice, so do everything you can to stand out from your competition and help that person on the other side to make an easy choice.

The tricky part about NYFW credentials? It's not enough just to have a press pass. You actually have to be invited to each show individually, and this part is up to the designers and their teams. In fact, you could skip the credentials altogether and simply contact each designer or brand asking for an invite, but that is a tad risky. Plus, the advantages of having the credentials are that they give you all-time access to the venue itself, plus guarantee your inclusion in the press list sent out to the designers, which is valuable all year, not just during Fashion Week. So if you have credentials, you will get at least a few invites automatically without having to request one. It's a great way to put your personality and blog on the map and even a way to be included in general press lists for those brands outside the fashion weeks.

Whether you have the credentials or not, when requesting invites from designers or brands, make sure to follow these tips:

- **Find the right contacts.** If you have credentials, you will be receiving the contacts list from the fashion week organizers. If you are reaching out without credentials, you can find all the contacts at the Fashion Weeks section of *ModemOnline.com*. Some designers handle their invites internally, so you will need to email the PR manager or director, but most hire an agency to handle their press list for the fashion week. Some of these agencies handle one show, while others, like BPCM, People's Revolution and KCD handle multiple clients. In this case, they create dedicated email addresses or phone lines for all invite inquiries. These days, most of them also use electronic event management system, FashionGPS, which makes it easier to manage press contacts. In most cases, if you are in the FashionGPS system for one company, you will be getting invites to several designers' shows they represent.

- **Include all the needed info.** If you are requesting an invite directly from a PR person via email, make sure to include the same info you included in the press application: blog URL, its focus, launch date, traffic numbers, audience demographics and your entire contact info—including phone, email and mailing address. Be brief and polite. Don't argue if you are declined, as in this instance it probably won't help.

- **RSVP in a timely manner:** Understand that most shows' seating charts are done days in advance, so make sure to RSVP as soon as you get the invite.

Lastly, if you do get your credentials, but don't receive an invite to the show you really wanted to cover, don't give up. Come early before the show and ask the PR person in charge of the check-in for a standing room ticket. In most cases, this is what you will get anyway as a newbie. It will give you a glimpse of the show, and if you can make a nice coverage out of this experience, you might be getting your seat next season.

This was my best kept secret during the first few seasons of NY Fashion Week I've attended. Even though I had my press credentials, the list of designers who invited bloggers to their shows back in 2007 was extremely short. So, before each show, I came early and introduced myself politely to the PR people in charge. I got standing room tickets in 80% of the cases, and most of them sent me the actual invite the season after. Sometimes the in-person contact does magic, and PR people need that validation to make sure you are a professional and committed to your craft.

These are the most important qualities you can bring with you to the fashion week, along with general humility. I see some bloggers at recent fashion weeks here in New York starting to feel entitled; sometimes they even make a scene if they aren't seated in a certain row. Remember that our craft is still a new territory for many fashion brands, and while some put bloggers in their front rows, others are still trying to navigate the space and decide who is who. Make their job easier by establishing connections early on, before the fashion week season. When it's time to send out their invites, your name will be on the right list.

Build Relationships with Brands.

While building your relationships with brands, be strategic: **learn to separate brands you love with brands you want to do business with.** It works just like dating—you don't want to necessarily marry the "hottest guy on the block"; you are better off getting into a relationship with someone you can trust and share similar values. It is important to pick your partners wisely when you are building your blog as a business for multiple reasons:

Most of the "cool" brands we tend to love have no money to spend on blogs. They either don't need to pay for marketing because they produce enough news to get your coverage, or they simply can't afford marketing. It doesn't mean you shouldn't cover them, just the opposite. They might provide you with some of the best, most unique exclusive content, but just be aware that these relationships probably won't contribute much to your bottom line.

If you want to focus on a long term career, it's better to start building relationships with more established brands. You want to work with people who will be in business years from now. We've seen many designers of the moment come and go, and while some created amazing works, they can barely earn you valuable readers or potential income. From a business perspective, you should always go for long-term relationships and build them gradually. Why aim for a longer commitment?

- It's much more cost effective to have long term relationships and not waste more time on getting a new client or campaign.

- It doesn't dilute your personal brand, as you are working with the same company.

I like comparing those relationships to dating with all its ups and downs. Managing those relationships is a huge part of being a blogger and requires great skill, which is a must for everyone who gets to the top and ends up making a living off blogging. I would love to share some of my personal experiences with you.

While blogging on fashion for the past few years, I've been "romanced" by many brands; many times, it included champagne and caviar. Some opted for long distance relationships; some for online dating only, while some chose the route of a "one night stand" to hit their monthly goals. But many used the advantage of my New York City location to take the relationship to the next level—meeting face-to-face, building a personal connection and "dating" over time.

From fabulous events with flowing champagne, delicious bites, fresh flowers, iconic performances and breathtaking views—many of them gave me unforgettable moments that no man in my life has managed to top. Add to that the feeling of being appreciated, included, respected, desired, and pampered, and you get the picture of a perfect romance that can last years, benefiting both sides.

Unfortunately, as in real-life dating, it doesn't always last forever. Many times I've seen situations where a specific blogger or entire group of bloggers suddenly find themselves left behind—the emails, invites and exclusives simply stop coming. Whether the brand was "burnt" by the experience, didn't see immediate results in sales or perhaps simply had to cut the resources, it's a delicate situation which might turn the brand's biggest fans into offended "exes." Make sure you don't become one.

My main lesson from this experience was to never take anything personally. Yes, my blog represents who I am, but there are many variables that affect a brand's decision whether to work with a certain blogger or not. Respect that and never let your emotions hurt your reputation.

Besides that, many brands still fear working with bloggers, and it usually comes down to negative stereotypes. The media sometimes has a negative fashion blogger portrait, which many of the industry people have in their minds when they think about us. I feel this portrait shows a narrow point of view, while the reality many of us know is much more diverse. Living in NYC and being lucky to personally know a pretty large number of bloggers, I noticed all of us come to blogging from different backgrounds and for different reasons, and while we do share one similar passion, the way we live it varies.

While blogging is evolving as a business and profession for many of us, I think it's important for brands to recognize the differences between various groups of individuals in the fashion blogging landscape in order to avoid stereotyped thinking.

Here are the ten most common stereotyped statements about fashion bloggers I found:

- **"Fashion bloggers are teenagers or people in their 20's."** For some reason, most of the bloggers that get press attention are pretty young. Young successes such as Tavi Gevinson and Jane Aldridge are names we keep seeing in the mainstream press, but the truth is, there are many bloggers in their 30's and 40's who rarely get the spotlight.

- **"Fashion bloggers are skinny, tall and picture perfect."** It might seem to the outsider that most successful bloggers are models who never made it. They are pretty enough to post their own editorial style photos, they are skinny, and sometimes even model-esque tall. One look at the homepage of sites like *Lookbooks.nu* or *Chictopia* is enough to get an idea of the stereotype. The fact is, we all come in different shapes and sizes.

- **"Fashion bloggers are loud and eccentric."** Some fashion bloggers do have loud and "out-there" personalities, but many are also strictly business people with backgrounds in everything from marketing to finance to human resources.

- **"Fashion bloggers are ego driven and attention seeking."** Not every fashion blogger is the subject of their own posts. Most actually invest lots of energy in covering the industry, designers, trends and everything that's happening—outside their own persona. They spend their own time and money covering events, researching subjects and looking for inspiration, just like reporters do.

- **"Fashion bloggers do it mostly for free swag."** I'm not saying that some bloggers don't have free products and clothes on their agenda. I've also seen what insiders are calling "cloggers," who seem to attend events only for the gift bags and who fight for goodies at industry events. But, I know that for the majority of us, it's just a nice bonus, and when it's given, it is politely accepted (and disclosed, of course).

- **"Fashion bloggers write from home, mostly in their pajamas."** As funny as it sounds these days, I recently met a fashion designer who seriously believed this. When I replied that I have an office where I blog wearing more than pajamas, he was genuinely surprised. Sure, some of us blog from home or home office, but the image of the pajama-wearing blogger doesn't do justice to many of us who are doing it professionally.

- **"Fashion bloggers love coupons, sales and discounts."** While some of the blogs out there are shopping and savings oriented, the majority of fashion blogs are similar to magazines in the sense that they are looking for newsworthy or inspirational content, and coupons aren't one of them. Besides that, the recession has created a serious overload of sale events and just because you decided to discount your merchandise by 10% on Tuesdays, it doesn't mean every blogger would love to share it with their readers.

- **"Fashion bloggers love any promotional events, especially those with free cocktails and gift bags."** Sometimes I'm surprised by many PR pitches assuming how little it would take to get bloggers to their event. They might not realize that in the city like New York, these days, bloggers are invited to cover several events every night and brands must be very creative and engaging to get their attention. They must build a personal connection first. Free champagne and goodie bags just don't cut it anymore.

- **"Fashion bloggers are amateurs who don't have appropriate degrees or education."** While not all bloggers have fashion or journalism degrees, some have relevant industry experience or similar degrees in communications or media. Many bloggers I know are actually working in the industry in various capacities and blog in addition to their jobs. Even more of them are college graduates and hold advanced degrees.

- **"Fashion bloggers don't use judgment, common sense or ethics before publishing content."** No, bloggers aren't professional journalists, but this doesn't mean they don't use common sense when covering news, reviewing collections or attending professional events. They are often driven by their personal opinions, which makes them much more risky for a brand than any "objective" mainstream coverage. On the other hand, the reward is much higher. When influential bloggers personally rave about a collection or a product, consumers trust them.

It's important to be aware of these stereotypes, so you don't fall into the trap of misconception. They might also explain some of the reluctance of the brands you are trying to work with, so you can try to position yourself differently.

Make a Dream List of Clients.

When strategizing your business relationships with brands, it's important to have a target list. Ask yourself, "if I could work with any brand in the world, who it would it be?" You would be surprised how many successful bloggers I asked weren't able to answer this simple question.

If you don't know who you want to work with, how will you attract them? Knowing who some of the brands are that you are going after as your business partners will focus you on building those relationships, and if you do it right, will eventually attract their business. They might decide to buy advertising on your blog, or work with you on a custom program. If that's not an option, at the very least you will be receiving their news or exclusive content that will attract more traffic to your blog.

Be proactive about these relationships. Instead of sitting and waiting for the opportunity to knock on your door, think strategically about how you can attract the ones you really want.

Start by making a short and a long list of your dream clients. I personally like to focus on retailers, as they have bigger budgets than a single brand. In most cases, it also won't create a conflict of interest with your editorial coverage, as retailers are carrying multiple brands. They are also more trusted and suitable for long term relationships. I would suggest your list contain one department store, one online retailer, one flash sale site, one beauty, one technology and a few lifestyle brands that would be among your dream clients. My dream list includes Saks, Rue La La, Jurlique, Hewlett-Packard, Virgin (I'm a huge Richard Branson fan), and lastly Louis Vuitton, a luxury brand I admire.

Once you've made your Dream Client list, start building your relationships, beginning with PR and social media. That way you will get on their radar, and hopefully, if the fit is right, eventually on their marketing plan as well.

If you are building a long-term career, don't compromise on the brands with which you are working. Yes, you have to start somewhere, but working with certain brands may eliminate the opportunity to work with one of your dream list clients in the future. This is especially true for luxury and high-end brands that are naturally more selective when it comes to where and how their name will be used, including the companies with which potential spokespeople might have been previously affiliated.

Knowing what you want and patiently waiting for the right opportunity will pay off if you build the basis for good relationships. I see proof of it every day in my business. Most relationships that bring revenue today are the ones I started one or two years ago and slowly built trust. Look at the big picture, have a clear client strategy, be proactive and you will be on the right path to working with your dream clients.

Blogger Inspiration: Q&A with Jessica Quirk of What I Wore.

How did you come up with the name and the focus for your blog?

I started my blog, *What I Wore*, in 2008 after a year of taking my daily outfit photo and posting it to the "wardroberemix" group on Flickr. I had been maintaining a personal blog during that time as well but felt like these photos needed a home of their own. I focus on personal style, which means almost all of the posts are based on what I actually wear on any given day. Additionally I post DIY (do-it-yourself) projects, sewing tips and New York Fashion Week coverage twice a year.

There are a lot of different kinds of personal style bloggers living in fashion capitals like New York, LA and Paris. These girls do an excellent job of showing off the runway style, but I think my blog's success has come from sharing a relatable, everyday style of getting dressed. I encourage my readers to mix investment pieces like shoes, handbags and denim with bargain buys and thrift store finds. I believe that everyone deserves to look and feel good and that it doesn't need to cost a fortune to do so.

Did you quit your job or other occupation to make more room for blogging?

When I first started What I Wore, I was working as a private label fashion designer in New York City. Each morning, I would set my camera up on a tripod or park bench and use a timer to capture my photos. I'd edit them before work, during lunch, or over the weekend. Now, my husband shoots all of my outfit photos and I've upgraded my camera.

The transition between a very secure desk job to the unpredictable income stream of an entrepreneur was scary to say the least (especially during a recession). Before I finally said farewell to my employer, I created a savings safety net to last six months. That was in May 2009, and I've been successfully working on What I Wore full time since then!

How did you build your audience?

I host my blog on Tumblr, which has played a huge role in developing an audience and following because of the social aspects of their service. It's quick and easy for your content to be shared with tens of thousands of people, reblogged and linked back to your site.

In the early days of my blog, there weren't a lot of communities or conferences educating bloggers on how to work with brands or what kind of traffic and audience was needed to start corporate partnerships and sponsorships. A blogger friend of mine told me that I needed 2000 daily visitors before I should ever think about monetizing my blog, and by the end of the first year I had amassed about 3000 daily uniques. Then, another friend told me I was in a position to turn the site into a business. At that point, I really had nothing to lose, so I worked out a media kit and started making connections and pitching small online boutiques.

What are some of the revenue channels for your blog?

My key revenue channels are product integrations and banner advertising. From my very first sponsored post, I've been very transparent about the relationship between blogger and brand, which is essential in maintaining authenticity. I only work with brands and companies that I would shop on my own including Timex, Coach, LOFT, Lancôme and Windows Phone. I love handmade jewelry and vintage clothing so I work with small businesses and Etsy sellers as well.

In the early days of What I Wore I did a lot of cold e-mails to introduce myself, my audience and pitch ways that I could partner with brands. Through networking and social media I've been able to establish new contacts, and the pitch process works both ways now. It's been especially important for me to learn to pass on the opportunities that aren't a perfect fit with What I Wore and I'd estimate that I only work with about 5% of the brands that approach me now.

I tailor all of my pitches to the individual brand with which I'd like to work, but I always start by sharing more of who I am, what my demographics are and how they're in line with the customer that company typically targets. I have both a PDF file and a link on my website with that information. The key numbers I always include are monthly page views and monthly unique visitors. I know from other research that my readers are women that span between teens and moms and are looking for real world ways to get dressed with an occasional splurge or special item in her closet. Once I've outlined that information, I'll lay out exactly the kind of post I'd like to put together for the brand including how many anchored links (to the homepage, e-commerce or Facebook) and the look and feel of the post. I'll wrap it up by outlining a budget proposal for the scope of work I've outlined and potential dates for the post to run.

Is there one piece of advice you can give to aspiring professional bloggers?

The most important advice I have for anyone wanting to pursue blogging full time is that this is a business and you need to treat it as such. I deal with accountants, lawyers, PR teams, accounts payable, programmers and readers on a daily basis. It's much more than "just getting free stuff" or getting invited to fashion shows. The bloggers who realize the business aspect is a huge part of running a blog full time are the ones who are able to make a living doing it.

Action Items.

- Connect with few of your readers via email and ask them for honest feedback on your blog, especially what features they like most and what attracts them to your blog. Establish a connection with your trusted fans and keep them posted on any new developments you are planning. This will allow you to use them as a mini-focus group every once in a while, which can be invaluable.

- Email a blogger you admire and ask for one piece of advice for your blog. Ask them to be honest and keep them posted on any improvements you make, especially if you follow their advice.

- Find an email address of a representative at one of the big PR companies who works with clients you are interested in featuring. Mention your blog's focus, audience and traffic, and politely ask to be added to their media list. Wait for their response before emailing anyone else, so you can adjust your pitch based on their feedback or questions.

- Research networking events in your area. Try to attend at least one event every month.

- Make a goal to attend Fashion Week in a major city. Build a budget for your trip, then research hotels and travel deals to make the trip more attainable. Reach out to local sponsors and offer them a mention in every live report you send from the event.

- Make a dream list of brands with which you would like to work one day. Describe in detail what kind of project you see them doing with you. Keep the list close to your work desk, and take a peek at it once in a while, adding more ideas.

Chapter 4: Revenue

In the previous three chapters, we've built a solid foundation for your blog, including strong branding, high-quality content, passionate readers and helpful industry connections. Now that all these pieces are in place, you are ready to start monetizing the business you've built. Of course, you might have been able to make revenue from your blog from Day One by placing Google ads or doing occasional sponsorships, but in order to build a serious business, you need to take care of its foundation first. Having all the elements and a clear revenue strategy in place will set you apart from the rest of the competition and allow you to go after bigger clients, larger budgets and eventually become a more successful business person.

Outline Your Strategy.

You might have noticed that the word "strategy" has been my mantra in this book. It is also my mantra in life. I subscribe to a belief that if you don't know where you are going, you will never get there. Applying it to your case and to the purpose of this book, if you don't know how you will make money from blogging, you will never make money from it.

Even if math was your least favorite subject in school, Excel spreadsheets put you to sleep, and the words "revenue strategy" scare you, it is essential to have a general idea of things like potential revenue channels and desired annual income. You can outline these ideas in your own words as part of your business plan, and come up with goals for each of the revenue channels, evaluating them on a monthly or quarterly basis and adjusting them accordingly. Why is it important to evaluate your financial goals often? Because, as you discover what works and what doesn't, you can minimize the time spent on activities that aren't profitable and shift your time to those things that will make you the most money. Here are some initial steps to help you decide on your overall revenue strategy:

1. **Define your assets.** Your blog is your media property, and you should treat it as such, whether you have a thousand visitors or a hundred thousand. It is important to get a scope of your assets in order to play the blogging business game. For example: you have a blog with X page impressions, an email list with X subscribers, a Twitter account with X followers, and a Facebook page with X fans. Get those numbers together and keep them handy in case they're requested and be sure to update them often. Even though your numbers don't define you as a brand, your potential advertisers should be able to measure your value in some way.

2. **Decide whether your persona is part of these assets.**
    Most fashion bloggers are open to putting their personality out
    there, and some are closing endorsement deals, ad campaigns
    and other opportunities based on their personality (and some-
    times even their physical appearance). If you are an expert in
    your domain or have carved a great niche, you might consider
    your personality one of your strongest assets for revenue genera-
    tion. If you've managed to create a following—even a small one—
    you might be appealing to some brands for profitable ventures.

3. **Decide which assets you want to monetize.** It might be a
    good decision not to monetize all of these assets at once. For ex-
    ample, you might decide that even though you are fine with run-
    ning occasional sponsored posts, you don't want to send out
    sponsored tweets. It depends on your audience, and some might
    be more tolerant than others. Just because you can utilize the as-
    set doesn't mean you should.

4. **Define your rules and boundaries.** They might be tough to
    decide on initially, but it's better to create those once than have
    ethical dilemmas every time a sponsor approaches you with an
    opportunity. If you are in the business of blogging, you need to
    have Editorial Guidelines and a Media Kit and both should be
    available online. It's easy to send people a link to these materials,
    and you can update both without resending to every contact. It
    presents you as a serious professional and eliminates possible
    unnecessary negotiations.

5. **Beware of giving out free services.** This is especially true for
    things like giveaways. Companies love offering giveaways and
    freebies to bloggers for a number of reasons: a) they "pay" in
    product, which in most cases is a low cost compared to the expo-
    sure they receive; b) they get free promotion, as if it was a dedi-
    cated sponsored post; and c) they get to engage with your readers

without doing much work. Not to mention all the promotion you syndicate for their giveaways on your Facebook, Twitter and sometimes through your email list. There is a lot of value in these channels, so don't underestimate them. Free giveaways allow brands and advertisers to use your voice and media property to reach your readers without compensating you personally for the service. If you decide to run giveaways on your blog, think about the following:

a) The value of the product. Is it an expensive item? How coveted is the brand? Does the product fit your niche and your readers' demographic?

b) Your involvement fee. Since your voice will be used to promote the product, how will you be compensated for the promotion? How many page views will the giveaway post generate during the promotion period and how does that translate to the cost?

c) The frequency. How many giveaways per week or month are you willing to run on your blog? How does it compare to the overall number of posts on your blog?

Once you have made decisions regarding these questions, be sure to create a giveaway policy and add it to your Editorial Guidelines, or at least have it in writing, once you're approached. It will strengthen your position as a serious business person and will add revenue potential.

6. **Set your rate card and stick to it.** Coming up with rates for your services is as difficult as setting your boundaries and editorial rules, but it makes your life easier by saving you from individual case-by-case decisions. Every channel you decide to monetize should have its own set price, whether it's public and part of your Media Kit or private and shared based on inquiries. Don't

be afraid to ask 20-30% more than you think you deserve—creative people tend to underestimate the fruits of their work, and sometimes you will be surprised how much people are willing to pay for them. It is important to stick to your rates, even if you have to say "**no**" sometimes (and you will have to do so, trust me). You will do a great service not only to yourself, but to your peers who operate in the space.

With that said, always take into consideration other variables, such as the brand name approaching you, the exposure you will get by working with a certain brand or a campaign, and your personal relationship with the brand. Sometimes adding a big brand name to your blogger resume can increase your own value and bring more future business, especially in the beginning of your career. We will discuss the rate card more in detail later.

7. **Learn to say "NO".** Before you say "**yes**" to an opportunity, even though it's not the right fit, think about why you started blogging in the first place. As an example, running non-relevant sponsored posts on your blog can turn off your readers. Placing a Wal-Mart ad on a high-end fashion blog may dilute the value of your blog and turn off potential luxury advertisers. There are only so many paid opportunities you can run on your blog, and only so many hours a day you can spend working, so when you accept opportunities that are not as valuable, you eliminate the possibility for better things to come. By accepting every opportunity that comes your way without filtering, you become a follower, rather than a leader of your own brand, and eventually dilute its value.

Think what *you* want to do, rather than whether you should accept something or not, so you can attract the right opportunities. There is power in our thoughts and desires, especially when we write them down.

In the first draft of this book, when I mentioned my dream list of clients, I had included a certain brand that I loved. By the time the edits were done, we were already working on a project together. In fact, they approached me about a month after writing down their brand name on my wish list. Don't underestimate the power of your dreams, and think long-term rather than how to make quick money; it pays off.

8. **Beware of bartering.** Even though it's a popular practice among bloggers, I strongly advise you to accept no forms of payment other than cash, checks and money transfers for the promotions you do on your blog. These days, some brands have a habit of paying bloggers with clothes and gift cards. By accepting them, you will never be able to build your blog as a business. Here's why:

    a) It's not scalable. What happens if you are get paid in shoes, and your traffic has increased? Do you ask for boots?

    b) It's unprofessional. Even if you only sell a sidebar ad for $50, you are still a service provider and should be treated as such by the brand. Service providers can't pay bills with gift cards and free pairs of jeans.

    c) It sets the wrong standard for the entire industry. See yourself as part of the blogosphere's microcosm and be responsible for the standards you set. It affects other bloggers and their potential revenues as much as it affects yours. When brands have experiences where they can obtain blogs by these low-cost means, it lessens the position of other blogs to negotiate in the future.

9. **Don't lose your essence.** And by that I mean many things: your personality, your writing, your daily portraits, your point of view, your editorial choices and much more. If the chase for

money/traffic/audience starts driving your blog's voice, it might be a good time to take a break and remind yourself why you started blogging in the first place. Even though revenue is important, your original voice and value mean more.

10. **Disclose your business relationships.** With all respect to money, I truly believe that authenticity is the highest online currency these days. Therefore, not disclosing relationships or misleading blog readers will never be in style. Think about this when you build your revenue strategy, and make sure your editorial voice stays the same, no matter how much your revenues increase. It's up to you to find the right balance between promotional and editorial content on your blog, as well as the way you disclose your sponsorships to your readers. Find the best format for you and stick to it so your readers can get used to it, and eventually see it as an integral part of your blogging strategy. After all, they understand that this revenue is necessary to keep you producing the high quality content you provide them each and every day.

Measure and Collect Your Data.

Before we get into the discussion on which services to offer and how to price them, you need to have a good idea of your various statistics and data. In fact, you should be able to recite these numbers in your sleep. Your traffic and audience demographics need to be monitored. If not on a daily, it should definitely happen on a weekly basis. Having your hand on the pulse will allow you react quickly during sudden traffic spikes and leverage them into consistent growth.

For example, you've been featured on another larger-scale blog or even traditional media. If you are aware of this incoming traffic from a particular source, you could target your fresh content for that particular audience and ensure they come back, subscribe or bookmark your blog. If you know about it only a week later, it might turn into a missed opportunity.

There are two ways to ensure you are on top of these cases:

a) Set up Google alerts on any variation of your name and the name of your blog. This way you will get almost instant notification via email every time your name or your blog's name is mentioned.

b) Check your traffic stats on a daily basis. Google Analytics is the best tool out there, and it's easy and free to install, but there are plenty of other measurement tools. Some even provide the live data metrics on the visitors currently reading your blog, so you can see your traffic in real time.

It's easy to set up your Google Analytics main dashboard with some of the most important metrics, so you can watch them every day:

- **Traffic volume.** This allows you to watch and compare your traffic by day of the week, so you can adjust your posting schedule accordingly. This also allows you to watch any changes, such as decrease or increase in the number of visitors, page views and search inquiries.

- **Traffic sources.** This is important to watch for the reason mentioned above, as well as for your own records. If another blogger features you or links to your content, it might be appropriate to express your gratitude in some way, such as email or tweet. You can see the top referring sites to your blog, and make a better decision on where to spend your efforts.

- **Keywords.** You can learn a lot about your traffic and audience by looking at the keywords people used to find your content via search inquiries. You can use this data to create more content on the subject and keep these passers-by on your site longer. For example, I discovered early on that posts including "How To" in their title get much more traffic than a similar post that doesn't include these words. One of our most read posts of all time is "How to wear a military jacket." Apparently, most people search in Google similarly to the way they speak. Simply adding phrases like "How to wear..." or "The best way to..." to your titles could increase their search value. I wouldn't have known that without getting this insight from my Google Analytics report.

- **Most popular content.** This needs no explanation—you simply must know which of your posts are most successful, so you can try to learn what made them so appealing to your audience and replicate their success. In the same case of the military jacket post, it gave me an idea to create more posts on this specific trend and attract an even larger audience. Sometimes it just helps to know what people are searching for. It can even give you ideas for future content. After all, we all want to be read.

- **Audience demographic:** This might be one of the most important data pieces you need to know as a content creator. You might be surprised to learn that the audience you think you are writing for is completely different from the audience actually reading your blog. By learning where they live, for example, you can tailor your content to be more local and relevant. With the tools available today, you can find out even more details, such as age, number of kids in household, average family salary and education level. Quantcast is the best tool with which to collect this data and is easy to install with just one piece of code on your blog. The difference between this tool and Google Analytics is that while Analytics has a private login for your eyes only, Quantcast information is available to the public, which means your potential advertisers can find and verify your stats and audience demographics. The fact that you are open about your numbers and audience can make advertisers more comfortable working with you versus another blogger.

Another way to measure your site's value proposition and analytics is by comparing it to other similar blogs. It's a good habit to watch your competition and learn from their successes. But again, be objective and don't get wrapped up in envy. Identify two or three blogs that are in your niche or that you consider to be competitors, and generate a competitive traffic report via Alexa. Although Alexa isn't the most trusted source in traffic measurement (it takes only a sample of the population, and the sites they visit varies from vertical to vertical), it's a great comparison tool. Just by looking at the comparison graph, you can get a pretty accurate idea of where your competitors are in regards to questions like: "did they see any recent growth", "how do their traffic and page views per user compare to yours", and "what are some of the top keywords attracting traffic to your competitors?" These are all the questions you can easily answer with one click on Alexa, and they could be extremely valuable for your content strategy.

While all these tools are great for your own use, what most of the big agencies and brands are using is either Comscore or Nielsen Reitings data. These are paid subscription services listing sites and networks of sites by verticals and provide an accurate snapshot of the site's unique visitors. Both have minimum traffic number that needs to be recorded in order to list a certain site. For example, even a medium size blog with 100,000 unique visitors might not be large enough to get a listing. In this case, Comscore's code needs to be installed on your site in order to be measured.

If you haven't signed an advertising agreement with any of the big networks, it's likely you are not listed on these services. The majority of ad networks request their publishers to "assign" their traffic to the network, so the publishers would appear under the network name, thus impacting the network's overall traffic. This is important for the network, so they are able to show a large number of unique visitors and go after bigger advertisers and budgets. However, from my experience, it also scares a lot of bloggers, as the term "assign your traffic" might sound like you are giving someone the rights for your property. In reality, it's not more than a listing, though an exclusive one. There is actually great value for a blogger to be listed in Comscore or Nielsen, even if as part of one of the networks. Remember, you can be listed only under one network at a time, which makes networks compete for an online publisher's exclusivity. More on this in the ad networks section.

Learn When to Ask for Money.

As social media continues to evolve, the lines between PR and advertising continue to blur to the point where social media marketing is considered a new form of free advertising on the web. PR and marketing agencies often see bloggers as free manpower, creating new types of user-generated, content-driven marketing campaigns for billion dollar brands. Brands that have succeeded in getting millions of free impressions across social media outlets pride themselves in cracking the secret code. Some agencies call it "earned media" and value it more than "paid media."

Bloggers, as influencers, are positioned high in this game because they are trusted sources that are able to spread information down the "influencer chain". Brands need them to push the message out and convince the masses. In addition, the recession has put lots of pressure on retailers, which now use their PR firms to not only create the buzz, but also increase the conversion of content to sales. More and more PR companies are pitching bloggers stories that push the limits of "free advertising." From sweepstakes and Facebook contests to advertising a special sale or a discount, some of these posts often look like oversized banner ads. These messages are usually part of a larger marketing campaign, where bloggers are just another vehicle for pushing the main campaign message. Instead of sponsorship fees, bloggers are often rewarded with products, gifts, free trips, cars or just with the prestige of being attached to a big brand name.

While in the long term those brands—which simply look to use social media and bloggers' influence as a free impressions pool—will need to rethink their model, it's very important for you as a blogger to recognize those cases and not to fall into the trap. Eventually, the oversaturated market will force these brands to adjust their strategy. The "free" model will have to evolve into more meaningful business relationships and you want to position yourself on the frontier.

While posting sale offers can definitely add value for your readers, especially if your blog's focus is budget shopping, it should be done in a tasteful way that doesn't compromise the editorial voice. A great example is *New York Magazine*'s blog, *The Cut*, which combines all sales offers in a daily text-only post without promoting one specific sale.

One of the consequences of posting promotional content is that, once you start, you get more sent your way, and it becomes a never-ending struggle to stem the tide of emails. You also largely eliminate the chances of these brands ever buying ad space or a sponsored opportunity on your blog. **Why would they ever pay you if you keep posting their promotions for free?**

The rules vary from blog to blog, depending on your niche, frequency of posting and your own interests. Take the time to develop your own set of rules when it comes to promotional content and stick to them, even if others have different opinions.

When in doubt, ask yourself a simple question: "Would *Elle, Vogue, Allure,* or *Marie Claire* ever post it?" If you place high standards on your blog, you will only be respected and your authenticity will never be questioned.

Don't be afraid to ask questions or voice your opinion to the people behind the brands when it comes to posting promotional content. If you feel uncomfortable with anything you are asked to post, it's important for them to know how you feel. Many brand promotions might be confusing or complicated, so be honest and communicate your concerns to your contact person. Even if the truth may be unpleasant to hear, they will be thankful for your feedback, as long as you can prove the point and provide constructive criticism.

For example, one day I received an email from a fashion brand I love and a PR contact I respect offering to participate in a video project for the brand, which was exciting but required me to spend a large amount of my own time and cancel other important things on my calendar. Instead of politely declining, I asked if it's a paid gig. I truly believe everyone should be compensated for their time, and especially if you work for yourself, your time is worth money. By hinting at compensation, I let the brand know that a case like that is considered a promotion, and it is expected for them to pay for service, whoever they end up choosing. In this instance, the brand didn't have a budget, and I decided to pass on the opportunity. However, they are now clear about my position and will try to plan on compensation for future projects. Saying "**no**" will pay off and eventually bring more opportunities that are in line with your working standards.

In another example, one of my favorite brands used my photo from their event in a styling competition on their Facebook page, running a sweepstakes around it. I felt uncomfortable with their use of my image in what should have been a paid promotional opportunity, even though I signed my legal consent to release the photo for any use at the event (another reason you should be very careful with what you sign). It was a social media marketing campaign, and my name and likeness were now part of it, without me receiving any compensation. I voiced my true opinion to the brand after the instance and asked politely to be given more information and disclosure the next time my photo would be used as promotional material.

The space is so new that even well-known brands are making mistakes and learning their lessons. It is your job to educate them on those mistakes; otherwise, they will never learn. Take responsibility for helping out the entire blogosphere to raise the standards and be active advocate for yours and your peers' rights when it comes to these types of social media marketing campaigns. By doing so, you will not only gain the respect of brands you are working with, but also help raise our collective bargaining power.

Learn When NOT to Ask for Money.

On the other hand, more and more PR companies are voicing their disappointment with bloggers who ask for money every time they are trying to pitch them an editorial story. Sometimes it looks to them like all the content posted on certain blogs is "bought" in some way. Asking a PR contact to pay you in cash or product for *every* item received from your relationship is not only inappropriate behavior that might cause you to lose the relationship altogether, but it also creates an unprofessional reputation in the industry.

Therefore, one of the most important things you should learn as a professional blogger is to **differentiate between editorial and promotional content.**

As a rule of thumb, you should know that most PR companies don't have budgets to compensate bloggers. They are hired to create editorial coverage and are paid a retainer fee to perform ongoing press outreach. They do have products or samples they can use for review and testing purposes, in which case, they will offer it to you. If you are interested in product samples, you should always have a good reason why you need to receive it before you can provide editorial coverage. It might make sense for beauty products, but sounds questionable in the case of a $4,000 jewelry piece. You need to be able to explain why it's necessary for you to receive the product. Asking for gifts is out of the question. Just as you will never ask your friends for a gift, why would you ask a brand representative to give you a product?

So far in my blogging career, I have received countless gifts and have learned to see them as a gesture of appreciation, even though several times I have declined expensive gifts that have made me feel uncomfortable. I always feel more comfortable with appreciation gifts and thank you notes sent to me *after* I posted my coverage, but in cases when I receive gifts that I love, I make an effort to thank the brand in an organic form via Twitter or by incorporating (and disclosing) the item into my ongoing coverage.

If you bring value to a brand, most will be thankful and will find a way to gift you or express their appreciation. If you have to ask for it, it means you are doing something wrong.

My last note: if expensive gifts and freebies are what attracted you to the craft of fashion blogging in the first place, I strongly advise you to reconsider your intentions. You won't be able to hide your motives for too long, and it will be impossible to build real, strong relationships with both readers and brands with this attitude.

Learn the Difference Between Advertorial Content, Sponsored Posts and Paid Reviews.

There is a lot of confusion in the digital space regarding these three terms: "advertorial," "sponsored posts" and a "paid review." Truth be told, all three are similar at the core: they describe content for which the blogger was compensated.

While previously some argued that paid posts are unethical, now it seems to be pretty much a norm, and every blogger who makes a living from their blog has probably posted sponsored content.

I believe in the idea of sponsored content and can prove that when it's done right, it brings lots of value to both the blogger and the brand. The trick is to follow these simple rules. The sponsored content needs to be:

- The right fit for the blogger's audience.

- The right fit for the blog's general focus.

- The right fit for the blogger's persona (in case of personal endorsement).

- Done tastefully, without overendorsing.

- Valuable to the blogger's readers.

- Fully disclosed.

- Done in moderation.

If you follow these simple rules, chances are that your readers won't object to sponsored content appearing on your blog occasionally. The ratio may vary from blog to blog, but I suggest no more than 10% of your content be sponsored (which makes it one out of every ten posts at the maximum).

Now let's look at the differences between the three types of sponsored content.

1. **Sponsored posts.** These are usually content that an advertiser provides to the blogger to post for a previously-agreed fee. A sponsored post might be customized to the blogger's own voice, but in general, it's simply posting information the brand wants to communicate to the audience. This information sometimes requires more text than you can fit into a banner ad, therefore, a blog post is a better format. The advertiser also gets more value by featuring their promotional message within the blog's stream of posts, therefore catching more attention. Additional value is gained by tagging the post just like other content, therefore making it appear in search results. Unlike a banner ad, sponsored posts usually stay on the site forever, after being archived with the rest of the content. A good example of a sponsored post would be a contest announcement by brand X. In this case, the blogger helps the brand drive traffic to their contest page or Facebook and the message is pretty straightforward, encouraging the readers to enter the contest and win prizes. Even though there is a value for the reader, this isn't necessarily editorial content most blogs will ever post. Therefore brands are willing to pay for this type of content being published across the blogs.

2. **Advertorial posts.** These posts are closest to a blogger's regular editorial features, but sponsored by a brand. They usually are written in a blogger's own voice, include the blogger's opinions or recommendations, and sometimes even include custom content the blogger has created for the brand. It definitely requires more involvement on the blogger's part, which means the bloggers are compensated for their time at higher rates. Here's a perfect example from a recent campaign: a well-known consumer camera brand approached Style Coalition to help find an influential blogger to create an advertorial post featuring their camera. We

suggested one of our bloggers who likes and does lots of her own photography and equipped her with the new camera to create an advertorial post featuring the photos taken with the camera. Since the main goal of the promotion was to highlight the zoom feature of the camera, we came up with a creative concept called "Zoom Into my Daily Life," which gave readers a sneak peek into said blogger's lifestyle, the objects surrounding and inspiring her on everyday basis, as well as showcasing the camera's abilities. It was a win-win campaign where the blogger got a creative paid assignment and was able to use it to create original content. At the same time, the brand got lots of value by being featured in a very organic, even though still disclosed, way. This is my favorite type of blogger-brand collaboration, and it seems to be the most popular type among smart, social media savvy brands these days.

3. **Paid Reviews.** This is my least favorite type of sponsored content, which I personally haven't done and have never advised anyone to do. I believe it compromises a blogger's integrity and hurts the readers' trust. Paid review is the cheapest, least creative, and, in a sense, laziest form of blogger-brand collaboration. As described in this book, there are so many ways brands can work with bloggers, why chose to simply buy their opinions?

     It reminds me of when a person goes to a psychic reader and pays them to tell their future. At that moment they usually have mixed feelings: on one hand, they want to know the truth, but they only want to hear the positive truth.

     When brands pay bloggers to write reviews for their products, they hope to hear the same positive truth. When a blogger doesn't like the product they've gotten paid to review, he or she has three choices:

     a) Write a positive review and lie to the readers.

b) Write a negative review and disappoint the sponsor.

c) Decline to move forward with the deal and return any compensation, which not only disappoints the sponsor, it creates a negative experience that can affect all bloggers moving forward.

You might argue that brands are willing to take the risk of a negative review when they approach bloggers. I would argue that no one would want to pay a blogger to critique their product negatively in front of thousands of loyal readers. Brands who want honest critique of their product pay people for anonymous surveys and private focus groups, never in public on a popular blog.

As a professional blogger, you have the freedom to choose which type of sponsored content makes you most comfortable. You should definitely have a clear idea and policy that you follow, so when brands approach you, you can respond with your personal policies and not be forced to play by anyone else's rules.

Learn Advertising Terms and Language.

Knowing the operational terms of your industry is an essential part of being a professional. As a blogger, advertising will probably generate the majority of your revenue, so you should get at least a basic idea of the terms ad networks and marketing representatives use. The essentials for communication are as follows:

1. **Ad impressions.** A statistic every time an individual ad is shown on a site's page. For example, if each page of your site displays a total of three ads, each page view will create three ad impressions. Usually impressions are counted and priced in thousands (see CPM reference below).

2. **Ad inventory.** The term refers to the number of total available advertising impressions on a certain site. For example, if your blog generates 100,000 monthly page views, and each page displays three ads in various sizes, your monthly available ad inventory will be 300,000 impressions.

3. **Banner ads pricing.** Most banners are purchased by advertisers on a CPM basis, which equates to the cost per thousand impressions. For example, if your site traffic generates 100,000 page views per month, you have one ad placement on each page and an advertiser bought banners on your blog for the price of 1$ CPM, you will earn a total of $100 a month. The average CPM prices vary and depend on the network with which you are working, the advertiser, category (fashion ads might have different prices than home décor), your blog's focus, as well as the market in general. In the past few years, CPM rates have seen a significant decrease and rarely cross $1 on average at generic ad networks. With that said, sites and blogs with solid branding and a devoted audience that are attractive to certain advertisers (espe-

cially luxury brands) could be getting $20 CPM and more. If you are working with one of the networks, most likely you will see the CPMs on the lower range, as they will deduct a commission for closing the sale and serving the campaign for you. If you book an ad campaign directly, you may receive a higher rate, since you will be cutting the "middle man" cost.

4. **Standard banner ads sizes and placements.** These ads come in standard sizes defined by IAB (Internet Advertising Board). Most blogs are offering 728x90, 460x60, 300x250, 160x600 and 300x600 pixel-sized advertisement placements, and these are the sizes with which most ad networks work. If you are serious about generating revenue from advertising, consider having at least two banner ad placements in your blog design. Most ad networks will require you to display the ads above the fold (in the top part of your page, before users need to scroll down.) The best blog design will have one 728x90 spot at the top, and one 300x250 or 160x600 spot in the sidebar.

5. **Rich Media.** This term refers to any banner ads which include interactivity. Sometimes they come in standard banner sizes, sometimes in custom forms and shapes. Those units are usually more intrusive and will therefore be priced about 100% higher than a regular advertisement. Sometimes they will also require special implementation on your part, which is another reason to request higher rates for these types of ads. The most common types of rich media include:

   a) **Video Units.** Sometimes those units look just like a regular 300x250 banners, only they contain a video file instead of a static image or flash animation. In most cases, the video doesn't start playing until a user clicks on it or at least the audio is muted so it doesn't interrupt the overall site experience. Beware of video units that play once the page loads, as they might provoke negative reaction among your readers. In this case, reach out to your ad network or advertiser directly, and ask them to change the ad settings.

b) **Expandable/Retractable Units.** In most cases these are activated when a mouse moves over them and can sometimes cover the entire screen. Most expand to double their size and uncover interactive content, which sometimes includes video and audio. Watch for those ad units and make sure they are not too intrusive for your readers to view your content or appear too often so as to disrupt their experience on your site.

c) **Pop-Up or Pop-Under Units.** While very popular in the late 90's and early 2000's, these units are often associated with lower-end brands and usually aren't welcomed by users, especially on fashion, beauty or lifestyle blogs. When considering an advertiser or an ad network, make sure these units aren't included in their campaigns.

d) **Floating Units.** These are used mostly for surveys and similar types of interactions. Their level of intrusiveness depends on the ad itself, its size and page location. In most cases, users won't be tolerant of these types of ads, even though they might be very profitable for you as a publisher.

6. **Full site takeovers and re-skins.** These are more aggressive forms of advertising that also require special work on the blogger side, as well relinquishing control of some of the blog's branding for the period of the campaign. In some cases, brands will ask to change your blog's background and visual appearance, which might not be well-received by your regular audience. This is a decision you have to make as a blogger, and the rates will usually include a flat fee and CPM price, depending on the opportunity.

It is necessary to understand all the various formats so you can make the most appropriate decisions regarding which advertising formats you will, and will not accept, on your blog. You will also be able to negotiate any special cases beyond traditional banners with your ad network. Remember, once you sign with a network, they will be able to feed ads to your dedicated placements in a relatively automated manner. Sometimes they will try to push intrusive ads that may hurt your readership. Negotiating in advance and including these cases in your agreement will allow you to either get a higher rate, or force the network to remove intrusive ads, or even terminate the contract in case of repeat violations.

By knowing and understanding proper advertising terms, you're not only protecting your interests and potential revenue, you are able to position yourself as a professional and earn repeat business. Brands, agencies and networks always prefer to work with an educated blogger and businessperson who understands the terms and is able to communicate with knowledge, saving both parties from potential misunderstandings and mistakes.

Choose the Right Ad Network.

It's often said that blogging is a lonely business. While being independent definitely allows you great freedom, it also forces you to wear many hats: content creator, editor, moderator, developer, photographer, model, sales person, business development, accountant and Chief Financial Officer. Many of these hats could be outsourced, without you spending any money. It might be worth the value of your time to consider joining an ad network.

One of the benefits of online advertising networks is that they operate on a commission basis, so they cut revenue share from the advertising sold on your site only after it's been sold. There are a variety of blogger networks, from big (representing thousands of blogs) to small (just a few blogs grouped together).

Advantages to joining a network of blogs:

- **It saves you time.** You don't have to do any advertising sales yourself, which allows you more time to do what you do best—create great content.

- **You don't have to deal with billing and payment collecting**, which might be a tedious task. The network will collect the payments, provide you with a monthly report and cut the payment directly to you.

- **Belonging to a prestige network of bloggers adds credibility to your blog.** Most networks are selective and have certain minimum requirements you have to meet. Passing their filter ranks you higher in the eyes of PR or marketing contacts who might want to work with you.

- **It adds visibility to your blog.** Most networks proudly display their publishers on a corporate website, not to mention inclusion in sales materials and presentations to clients. Some-times advertisers will get introduced to your blog for the first time through the network, and this might lead to deeper rela-tionships in the future.

- **It can bring opportunities besides banner sales.** Most ad networks are expanding their offerings to sponsorship opportun-ities and deeper engagements with brands and by joining a net-work you will be exposed to these opportunities. When consider-ing a network, inquire what other types of sponsorships and campaigns you could potentially work on together beyond the banner ads.

- **You get to work with bigger brands.** Most brands aren't open to the idea of working with individual bloggers. They prefer to deal with a larger network, representing multiple blogs, where they can either choose several blogs to work with, or run their campaigns across the entire network. That way, they don't have to negotiate and contract the blogger directly, which reduces op-erations on their part.

Now that you understand the advantages of belonging to an ad net-work, when is the right time to join? The answer is simple: join if you have an opportunity and it feels right. If you are approached by a net-work, it means they think you could be a valuable property to represent.

If you are not yet in this position and would like to reach out to a few networks in order to be considered, try to estimate your assets first to see if you fit their requirements. All major ad networks have minimum re-quirements, mostly referring to your site's traffic. In my opinion, if you haven't hit 25,000 monthly page views yet, it might be best to focus on increasing your traffic before you reach out to a network.

The more traffic you have, the stronger your negotiating position will be, and you will be able to broker a better deal. It also might not be worth your efforts to monetize such low traffic through banner ads, since, based on the industry averages, you won't hit even $100 in monthly revenues.

The decision of which ad network to join is a very important one in a blogger's career. Most of the networks will require some sort of exclusivity and a long-term commitment, which may range from one to three years. It's a long time in blogging world and you have to be wise in this decision.

What to look for in an ad network:

- **Check their list of publishers.** Are these reputable blogs? Are they bigger than you? I always try to join groups that have people more successful and profitable than me so I can learn from the best. However, there is also an advantage to joining a network with smaller blogs than yours, because chances are, you will get more opportunities by being one of their larger publishing properties. Just make sure your network has at least a few blogs with whom you will be proud to share company.

- **Look at their list of advertisers.** What are some of the brand names with which they work? These are usually listed on network's website in the Clients section, but sometimes those sections don't have the most up-to-date information. The best way to find out is to visit one of the blogs they represent and look at the ads displayed on that blog. Sometimes you will be surprised by the lack of connection between their promises and the reality.

- **What is their main focus?** Does this network specialize in the fashion, beauty or lifestyle vertical? Just because the network is big and they successfully represent, for example, gadget blogs, it doesn't mean they will be able to sell advertising in the fashion vertical.

- **What is this network's track record?** We operate in a small industry, where rumors run and bloggers often talk amongst each other, exchanging opinions and experiences. Reach out to a few people who worked with the network in the past and try to find out why they left. In addition, reach out to current members and find out whether they are happy. Things change quickly in the digital space, and networks that weren't very successful last year might be doing much better at this moment.

- **What kind of services do they provide?** Will you have a dedicated account manager with whom you can communicate in case of emergencies such as inappropriate or intrusive ads? Most big ad networks are too busy to provide such personal service, and at the same time, smaller networks sometimes don't have enough staff to respond in a timely manner. It is important to understand what kind of communication and access you will be getting. I've found this factor of personal service is very important to the majority of bloggers with whom I've worked, and it's the reason I provide personal service to Style Coalition members. It gives them confidence and reassurance that they are working with a trusted network, and their blog and revenue will never suffer because of lack of response.

- **What kind of commitment or guarantee are they willing to make?** Make sure you are not the only one who is giving in this relationship. You are basically putting your revenue source in their hands and giving them a certain control over your media property, so make sure they make some guarantees to serve you best. It's hard to get a monetary guarantee from ad networks, especially if you are in the beginning of your blogging career. However, it doesn't mean you can't request to include target numbers or goals in your agreement. It will not only provide a clear picture of what you can expect from the network, but it will also allow you to terminate the relationship in case those promises are not met.

- **Can they back up their promises?** While you want to trust your future partners, it's okay to ask for proof of their promises. This could be an advertising order from a client or recent report. These documents don't have to expose confidential information, but they should give you a proof when you are in doubt and when further evidence of their claims, such as member recommendations, couldn't be found.

- **Does it sound too good to be true?** Like everything in life, if it does sound too good to be true, it means something is probably wrong. The advertising industry works based on standards and cross-industry averages. If your research shows that the average CPM price most networks are offering stands at around $3, but a certain network promises you $20, they might be over-promising. In my career and experience of running an ad network for the past few years, I can say in full confidence that most networks over-promise in order to sign you on.

  My strategy is usually the opposite—when a blogger comes to me and tells they have a better offer on the table from a competitor, I advise them to look carefully at the agreement and never try to convince them to join our network instead. If they do, they will never be happy, as they would always think about that better offer they rejected. From my experience, most of them come back a few months after they signed with a competitor and complain that none of these promises have been met. From that point, I feel more comfortable working together as I know the blogger has realistic expectations and learned something from past mistakes. In general, I find the "under-promise, over-deliver" approach works much better. This is the approach I followed creating Style Coalition. Today, most of our bloggers are making two to three times more money than they originally expected, and they are happy with that surprising fact. I have a loyal group of customers (bloggers) who trust me, which is the biggest currency you can ask for as a business person.

Unfortunately, the majority of people working for ad networks have their own goals to fulfill, which usually relate to their overall traffic numbers, so the more bloggers they can sign, the better they look in the eyes of potential clients and competitors. Blogger interests aren't always on top of their agenda, and because the number of new blogs popping up grows every day, they don't feel the pressure of providing good service.

Watch out for these red flags when you are choosing your partners for an ad network. Make this long term decision carefully and seek legal or business advisors, if you can. It is one of the most important revenue decisions you will make, with long-reaching effects on your profitability.

Familiarize Yourself with Basic Legal Terminology.

Even though the complexities of running your own business usually require lawyer involvement, I find it extremely important to be familiar with the basic legal terms and standards.

Understanding legal terms can save you a lot of money because you're able to do most of the preliminary work yourself, meaning that you will only have to seek professional legal expertise when the situation calls for it.

For example, if you are negotiating an agreement with an ad network, you will have to sign a contract eventually. If you know to read agreements and understand basic terms, you will be able to ask the right questions and negotiate most of the points yourself, and only have your lawyer review the final version once you are ready to sign.

In the case of a completely new agreement written from scratch, it is helpful if you come prepared with bullet points and a general description of the project or partnership. Once you agree upon them, draw up the initial document and only then involve your lawyer for further additions and necessary advice.

Remember, some agreements fail and never get signed or executed, so at least in this case you won't be paying the lawyer's bill. Bottom line: pay for legal help only when you are ready to sign and have already agreed upon the basic terms of an agreement. In the case of standard agreements like non-disclosure, confidentially, or project agreements, there might be no need for a lawyer if you understand the basic terms.

Legal services are pricey, so make sure your issue or a contract is worth paying the bill.

My personal rule of thumb goes: seek legal advice only if there is money or potential revenue at risk. An ad network contract is definitely one of those cases. As an individual blogger you unfortunately have a disadvantage in regards to your size, whereas networks are usually big corporations with lawyers on staff who make sure to protect their own interests. Many of the ad network agreements I've seen in the digital space are full of pitfalls and potential complications you should be aware of. These are some of the most important things to which you should pay attention:

- **Exclusivity.** The most important thing is defining your relationships and the levels of exclusivity. Simply put, what are you allowed and not allowed to do with other parties under this agreement? In case of ad networks, some will only work with you on a campaign basis and will allow you to work with others. Some will request complete exclusivity in everything related to your media property. Some will require you to sign off your traffic to the network on Comscore and Nielsen Net Ratings—a common practice among most ad networks. You should be aware of the exclusivity levels so you never breach the contract, even unintentionally. You should also feel comfortable giving up exclusivity to a certain network, because this means they will be fully in charge of your ad revenue.

- **Contract term.** Another important point is how long these relationships will last. Most networks will want at least a one-year contract and some may require two or three years. There are multiple reasons why networks are always pushing for a long term contract. First, they spend some effort on their part to sign an agreement, set up your account in their system—legal, billing, ad serving, and other operational procedures. Second, the sales cycle takes on average between 3-6 months from the moment of proposal to the moment when the campaign is actually running, meaning it might take you a few months to see the results of their effort on any custom programs you are included in.

- **Renewal term.** Most agreements include an auto-renewal paragraph, to make the procedure of renewal easier on both parts,
  and save on additional legal fees. If both parties are happy, the
  agreement renews automatically. In case of any changes, or termination, there is a deadline for notice which will usually be at
  least 30 days to allow parties to renegotiate.

- **Out clause.** In what cases can either party cancel the agreement? How long of a notice are they required to give? Every
  agreement should include this section, allowing you to terminate
  in case of non-performance. This is why setting goals and
  benchmarks is very important, which brings me to my next point.

- **Guarantees.** Most networks usually want to stay away from any
  guarantees on their part, especially monetary. Truth be told, it's
  hard to predict the revenues in this newly developing market,
  and they may vary from month to month (for example, January
  is known to be the lowest revenue month in advertising). Since
  the networks operate on a commission basis, they don't want to
  take the risk of having to pay publishers out of their pocket in
  case of low sales. However, you can request a performance guarantee, mostly to allow you to terminate the agreement in case of
  low sales figures.

- **Requirements & Obligations.** What are some of the requirements from you, as a publisher, besides the exclusivity? Are
  you required to display any special logos, links, or widgets on
  your site? Most networks require just displaying their logo, but
  some may require you to post their content widget on your sidebar, which may take space from other ads or content. Do you
  have the right of refusal for any of the sponsorship opportunities? Are you able to ban certain ads from displaying on your
  site? Are you required to notify your network in case of other
  campaigns you sell directly? For example, one of the networks

I've worked with allowed us to generate our own direct sales for advertising, but required us to get an approval for each direct sponsor to make sure they don't pitch the same brand.

- **Payment terms.** Make sure it's clear how, when and how often you will get paid. Know whether it's a check or direct deposit, a monthly or quarterly payment, and on which date it will be issued. How soon after collecting the ad revenues will you be paid? Some networks pay on a Net 60 or 90 day basis, and some even take 120 days to issue your first check. You should be aware of these legalities so you can plan your revenues accordingly. In addition, in case of the breach of one of these terms by the network, you may demand a termination of your agreement.

These are just the basic terms that are usually part of every advertising, partnership or representation agreement. Knowing what to look for will help you negotiate your contract without being overwhelmed by legal terms, even without professional help.

Remember, the biggest challenge in crafting a legal document is making sure they are balanced and not one-sided. Both sides need to set goals and describe the value they bring to the table. This is really the key to any successful partnership.

Develop Affiliate Revenue Channels.

The main strength of blogs, especially in the fashion vertical is the power of their recommendations and their ability to influence sales. If you've managed to develop a strong following that trusts your opinions, they will buy the products you recommend. When it comes to affiliate revenue, what's important is not necessarily your traffic numbers, but the levels of engagement your readers display on your blog. Do they click the links of the products you recommend? Do they follow your advice? Do they share their finds with other readers via comments? If the answer is yes, you might be able to generate revenue through affiliate sales.

Affiliate revenue is performance-based commission on any sales you generate through your blog. Affiliate advertisers recognize your readers through unique links they provide for your blog and compensate you based on the percentage of overall sales when your readers shop for products and services via this link.

Most affiliate advertisers use affiliate networks since it's the easiest way to plug their product list into the system and make it available to publishers. Each product gets a unique link with a special tracking code, so the publishers can embed it every time they refer to this product. The special affiliate link tracks and records—everything from the number of clicks to the number of purchases made from the specific source—in this case, your blog.

You get paid only after the purchase has been finalized on a commission basis, which varies depending on the retailer. The commission can be a fixed amount (e.g., $10 per sale) or a percentage amount (e.g., 10% of the total sales value). Besides the potential revenue, affiliate links are actually a great way to find out the conversion on your product recommendations. How many of your readers click through your links? How many love your recommendations so much that they actually purchase the product right away? This information can be valuable to you as a content creator and give you great insight into your reader's shopping habits.

While the list of affiliate networks is pretty large, the most known among them are LinkShare and Commission Junction. Both work in similar ways, and only the list of their retailers varies. You may open a publisher account on a several networks, although it would be easiest to pick just one service that maintains relationships with the retailers that make most sense for your audience.

Once you've created an account on your affiliate network's site, you may have to apply for certain retailers to allow you list their products. Some retailers approve publishers automatically and some (usually more high end ones), have strict policies and only approve bloggers on a case-by-case basis. If you are denied by a certain retailer with which you desire to work, try reaching out to their affiliate marketing manager directly. Asking to be added to their trusted list of publishers might be a better strategy.

After being approved by a certain retailer, search their list of products and gather a unique list that will help you in tracking your sales for that particular product. For example, if you are working on a post featuring white dresses, it will make sense to search for the products via your affiliate network and use affiliate links that will generate revenue from every dress you sell through your recommendations on this post. Even if you earn about five percent of the sales, it could still turn into nice income, especially if the dress has an expensive price tag and your audience responds well to your recommendation. Affiliate revenues vary from blog to blog, but some manage to make a six figure income from this channel alone. Yes, it requires some work and perhaps time spent finding out what works for your readers, but once you've found the formula, it can definitely be profitable.

My biggest affiliate revenue to this date came from recommending a dress similar to the one by Narciso Rodriguez that Michelle Obama wore on Election Night. I made a list of four black and red dresses and attached affiliate links to each. The post was extremely successful—both among my readers and with the immense search inquiries that came in the morning after. I sold more than twenty dresses via the affiliate links in one day and continued to use the same approach for future posts of this kind.

While bloggers who choose to juggle editorial content and revenue generation will have to make many choices, one important piece of advice is to make sure your affiliate sales don't start dictating your content. It's easy to get swayed by what generates money versus what keeps your blog focus on track.

Monetize Video.

If you have managed to successfully develop good quality video content, this may become a great additional revenue channel for your blog. The best way to monetize video is by creating a series format for your video posts, which is consistent in content and released with a certain reliable frequency. You will need to create at least a few episodes before you can approach sponsors or be able to negotiate distribution deals. Five to ten episodes could give a great idea about the direction of your series, but sometimes even a well put-together "pilot" episode could be enough. There are few ways to monetize video online:

- **In-video ads.** These include pre-roll and post-roll commercials, as well as layover ads that appear within your video content. They are usually added by the distribution platform automatically and it's up to you as a content creator to opt in or out. An example of such platform is Blip.tv, which specializes in original personal shows. While uploading your video onto the Blip.tv platform, you are asked whether you would like to add pre- or post-roll commercial. For their bigger content creators, Blip.tv negotiates individual sponsorship deals.

- **Display media surrounding the video.** Some platforms will share the revenue for the banner ads displayed on your video page. Blinkx is one of them and has been successfully generating revenue for some of my own videos, creating a nice passive revenue stream for me. YouTube also offers a revenue share program for videos that generate substantial amount of views.

- **Integrated sponsorships.** The same way you monetize your written content by offering advertorials and sponsored posts, you may offer sponsorships for your video content. A few ways to integrate sponsorships into your videos:

- ○ **"Brought to you by..."** You could find a sponsor for your entire video series or specific episode and either add a slide at the beginning of the video with a company logo or mention the sponsor at the beginning of your video. It might be the easiest way to monetize your video content, which also guarantees exposure to your sponsor. Sorel shoes sponsored our entire fashion week coverage back in February 2010 by attaching their name to every single video episode we created that week. Their logo was prominently featured in the first frame which said, "NY Fashion Week coverage is brought to you by Sorel." The sponsorship not only covered the production expenses on the exclusive content our readers were excited to see, but created additional revenue.

- ○ **Product placement.** You may sell certain product placements in your video. Different types of companies might be interested in being featured in your video in some way, from location sponsorship (restaurants, stores) to beverages and gadgets. Think about what brands appeal to your audience and go after them.

- **Branded content.** This is where you create your entire content around a specific brand. In this case, they may give you certain guidance and request specific content to be added or mentioned down to the writing of a script. In this case, you, of course, have to feel comfortable with the assignment and be able to relate to the brand in some meaningful way. This is a very popular and growing trend among brands that are looking for authentic content to replace their usual commercials and engage deeper with the influencers (bloggers) and their audiences.

  A great example of this type of campaign would be the most recent collaboration between Lancôme and our Style Coalition bloggers. Twenty of them were invited by Lancôme to create their own one-minute long films, inspired by the different colors of Lancôme's newest eye shadow palettes. Bloggers were given full freedom to dive deep into what inspires them and their lifestyles with minimal guidance from the brand. The result was twenty artistic video pieces, each showcasing Lancôme's colors in a different way and creating great original content for the bloggers to share with their readers.

I believe we will see more video collaborations between brands and bloggers in the near future and those with on-camera experience, and especially those with their own video content, will have a great advantage for monetizing.

Create Your Rate Card.

Now that you've decided on the revenue channels you would like to develop, you have to come up with your rates. Even though the market dictates its prices and you will be offered a certain amount for most opportunities, some will ask you to name the price.

In fact, the most common question I get asked by bloggers is, *"How much should I charge?"* The difficulty of pricing the craft of a blogger lays in the question of the different variables that define the price.

For example, if you decided to get paid based on an hourly rate, it means you will never be compensated for the foundation and behind-the-scenes work you do to build your brand and your media property. It might only take you one hour to write and post sponsored content for a brand, but what about three years of hard work you put into developing this business, which is what this brand is taking advantage of now?

If you are measuring sponsored content by a CPM (cost per thousand views) rate, which is most common in the online advertising space, you might under-price yourself. The issue with this kind of pricing is that it's usually used for banner ads, so when it comes to custom content, video, or personal engagements, your monthly impressions are not necessarily the variable that needs to count. Sponsored content usually gets much more exposure and real estate on your media property, as opposed to a banner, which your readers are trained to skip in most cases. It also takes your time to create and customize content.

The most appropriate measurement would be to come up with a project or post fee, which raises the question of how you come up with the right number.

In most cases your fees would be a combination of the amount of work and your personal involvement needed for the project (hourly rate), your audience size (CPM) and the overall value you will be providing to the sponsor.

Lastly, there is what I would like to call an "opportunity cost," which is the number of sponsored engagements you are able to do per month. This is limited for multiple reasons:

1. You don't want to overwhelm your readers with sponsored content.

2. You have limited time on your hands.

3. You don't want to be involved with too many brands, especially if they are competitors. By working with brand X you might eliminate the possibility of working with brand Y for that time period or even beyond. By "lending" your name to a brand, you will be associated with it for a certain time, so calculate that into your costs.

As an example, let's say your blog generates 250,000 page views a month with 50,000 unique visitors, and you've done one or two other brand collaborations, but nothing too big. Brand X approaches you with an opportunity to help them judge and promote their fans contest for the period of three months, which will include two dedicated sponsored postings on your blog, a guest post on their Facebook page, your brand name used in conjunction with the contest, and the hosting of the contest finale event to meet the winner. In this case your fee would be a combination of all these things described above. You may charge $500 for each sponsored post on your blog, another $500 for the Facebook post and feature; and $1,000 for event hosting, not including travel expenses, which are paid separately. So you might be looking at the total fee of $2,500—a reasonable sum for a brand to pay, yet attractive for you as additional income for your blog.

Other variables that might affect your rates are the market itself, your competition and current marketing trends. You simply can't ignore it and stick to some numbers you decide, because you will be losing opportunities that others might be taking on. Learn to be flexible and shift based on market information to ensure that you stay current in your pricing strategy.

In most cases, you will be offered certain compensation and will have to decide whether or not to accept it. While evaluating opportunities, think about these aforementioned points, but also consider any added value that this opportunity might have. Some sponsored campaigns provide a huge exposure and press coverage, which is worth X amount of dollars on its own. As mentioned earlier, especially at the beginning of your career, adding a big brand name to your blogger resume might be very beneficial, and attract even more future sponsors.

The best way to approach your rates is by creating your internal rate card to which you can refer each time you are approached with an opportunity. The advantage of keeping it private is that you can adjust your rates based on a project and remain competitive. Share the rate card with a marketing representative if requested, but know that it might cost you certain opportunities.

For example: if your rates are more than 50% above their budget, they might skip you and offer it to other bloggers. If your rates are way lower than what they thought to offer, you will be losing potential revenue. Since the blogosphere is still the Wild West, and there aren't many industry standards, my advice would be to keep your Rate Card internal and only quote your prices when the opportunity for revenue arises.

Creating a rate card is an essential step in building your revenue strategy. Even if you end up charging different fees for promotional opportunities, it creates goals that can guide you and allows you to estimate your potential revenue in the long term.

Create a Media Kit.

A media kit is your number one marketing tool, and, as such, requires considerable thought and effort to put together. It's worth investing in a few professionally-created pages or presentation slides that will make your response to every sponsor or advertiser inquiry very professional and easy. **This presentation is a must if you are serious about turning your blog into a business. This is the showcase of your talents, abilities, reach, and value as a blogger and influencer.** A great media kit can ramp up your value and create a more professional impression of you.

Your media kit is the language marketers speak, which will make working with you easier and more likely to succeed. If PowerPoint isn't your strongest skill or you're easily intimidated by graphics and design, go for a simple and functional look. In fact, this is where less is more. All you need to grab marketers' attention are short, bullet point descriptions and key stats.

Here are the essential elements of every media kit:

1. **Introduction.** This can be as simple as one paragraph describing your blog's focus, target audience, launch date and size. Example: "Sweet16 Blog focuses on a plus size fashion for teenage girls with a goal to solve their collective issue: the ability to expand a narrow choice of trendy, young looking clothing. The blog was launched in 2010 by Laura Smith and is today a destination for young women across the country, reaching more than 100,000 monthly unique visitors."

2. **About you.** Who are you as a blogger? List your professional background, any relevant job experience and the reasons you started this blog. You don't have to make it sound like an official bio. Your personal story relevant to your blogging experience

could add a nice touch. Mention where you are located and whether you have any special local reach or focus. More and more advertisers are looking to reach regional audiences, so sometimes being located in a place not saturated with bloggers can make your position even stronger.

3. **Credentials**. If your blog has been featured or mentioned in a magazine, other large blog, a newspaper or on TV, this is the place to mention it. If you belong to any prestige network or organization, state your affiliation. A raving review or a quote will do a great job as well. Show that you are a trusted source of information, acknowledged by others.

4. **Target Audience.** Describe the typical visitor to your site, their average age, average income, location, education, habits and any other insight you might have. This data is available via Google Analytics and Quantcast, which we discussed earlier in the Data Measurements section.

5. **Traffic Stats.** Include your number of unique visitors, page views and the number of ad impressions available on your blog. If you publish a newsletter or have a RSS feed, list the number of subscribers. Include the number of followers on other social media channels, such as Twitter, Facebook and YouTube (if you publish videos.) All this info helps the marketers to evaluate you as a media property.

Don't ever lie about or pad your traffic numbers. It's so easy to find out your real traffic numbers in this online world and most marketers have access to this data. If there is a big gap between the numbers they have and the numbers you provided, this might make them trust you less as a business person and possibly even jeopardize your chances of working with them. What do you do if your traffic keeps changing month-to-month? Take an average of your last three months and note that your traffic numbers are based on data collected for that certain time period.

6. **Advertising and sponsorship opportunities.** In the next few slides, try to list the various opportunities available on your blog for advertisers and sponsors. As mentioned above, you don't have to include prices, but including examples and screenshots of real campaigns you've done would be very helpful. If you haven't yet done campaigns, create a mockup using a fake brand or one of your favorite brands, but make sure to state clearly that the brand name was used for illustration purposes only and doesn't indicate a real campaign.

7. **Value for brands.** This might be the most important slide of your media kit and, as I learned from my personal experience, the most important thing in selling any campaign. Describe the value an advertiser or a brand will gain from working with you or obtaining exposure on your media property. What can you bring to the table? An original voice, state-of-the-art photography, an audience trusting every word you say, engaged readers who passionately comment and share their opinions, maybe even all of the above? Find out what will make you the ultimate choice for brands and make you stand out from the millions of other blogs.

8. **Case Studies.** There is nothing that sells better than showing a potential sponsor the results of your previous successful relationships with other brands. Besides making them feel more comfortable to work with you, you can actually show them what they can expect from you and set appropriate expectations. If you haven't done any campaigns or can't yet show results, approach a friend or a relative who owns a business relevant to your audience and offer to run a free campaign for them in return for using their name and campaign numbers as your case study. You can even try reaching out to some of the more established brands

and hope they would jump on the free marketing opportunity. Don't do it more than once: one case study is enough to illustrate your value, and you don't want to set a bad precedent by working with brands for free. If you are clear that you will provide these services for free, one time only and for case study purposes only, you might even gain your first future paying client in case the campaign is successful.

9. **Contact info.** Make sure to state email, address and phone number on your media kit, just in case it gets forwarded to someone else without your original email.

Of course, you can add anything else that you think might be relevant to your media kit, but I find that concise presentations make a better sale. Clear, clean documentation that is succinct makes it easy for people to understand what you do and how they can work with you. This isn't the place to get creative and try to come up with your very own version of something as standard as a media kit. When it comes to speaking the language of marketers, try to be as clear as possible. Don't try to reinvent the wheel.

Think about your media kit as the ultimate showcase of your abilities and make sure it represents your true value. Send it to a few friends or business associates to gain their feedback when creating it and ask if it makes you look attractive for potential sponsors. Finally, make sure to update your media kit every few months, especially if your traffic grows or you add more campaigns you can showcase. If you take the craft of marketing yourself seriously, others will do the same.

Discover Other Revenue Opportunities.

The revenue opportunities described earlier in the book are just common ways to generate revenue from your blog. The truth is there are many other revenue streams you can develop based on your blog. This is the part when you have to get creative and think a) what make sense for your blog and its niche, and b) how you may differentiate yourself from other bloggers by offering unique opportunities and services no one else does. These may be media sponsorship opportunities on your blog or something that relies on your personality.

For example, if you have a special Friday column talking about a particular subject, you may offer potential sponsors the opportunity to put their name on that column for a certain period of time, to essentially brand it. If it's a contest or a poll you run among your readers on a monthly basis, you may offer contest sponsorship to a brand. A gift guide or holiday special post can be another opportunity that brands would love, as they always plan promotions around the holidays.

In addition to your blog, if you position yourself as a true expert of your blog's niche subject matter, you may tap into countless personal engagement opportunities. Some common examples include:

- **Consulting engagements.** Brands or agencies might want to hire you on a project basis to help them to better understand your audience or your niche. Brands love hiring bloggers to help them with their own social media initiatives, as bloggers seem to know the ins and outs of online marketing and social media audience engagement better.

- **Speaking opportunities.** Sometimes you might be asked to speak about your experience and share your expertise in public. Speaking engagements might range from professional conferences to corporate functions and consumer events. Even though initially most of your public speaking could be done in trade for increased publicity, if you develop strong public speaking skills you will be able to charge for these services in time. In case of corporate functions or when you are invited to speak on behalf of a certain brand, you might be eligible to receive compensation for such an engagement.

- **Event hosting.** Brands love an authentic connection to their consumers, and who better to help them than an influencer who identifies with them? Bloggers with substantial audiences are hired to host local and national events, just like magazine editors have traditionally done before them. When you are hosting an event for a brand and your name is used in conjunction with that brand name, don't be afraid to request compensation or at least some form of monetary commitment, which may include, for example, media buy on your blog.

- **Acting as a spokesperson.** If you are building your brand relationship right and position yourself as a trusted source of information, brands might want to use you as a spokesperson in the future. We've seen bloggers and YouTube sensations inking annual deals with global brands, and I predict we will see even more of these types of partnerships happening in the future. Even though bloggers aren't Hollywood celebrities, sometimes their engaged audiences online are almost as large as a celebrity's respective number of fans. Bloggers can be more authentic sources of information than celebrities, not to mention much less expensive when it comes to endorsement deals and spokesperson appointments. These engagements don't necessarily have to be long-term global deals. They can be as simple as featuring your recommendations on a brand's Facebook page.

Nine West, with whom I've built great relationships over the past couple of years, invited me to be the "featured expert" on their Facebook page for the 2010 Holidays. I made my recommendations for the "It" accessories from their Holidays collection, and wrote a short piece telling their fans about the season's hottest trends. Even though it wasn't a full blown spokesperson opportunity, I was, in a way, Nine West's Facebook spokesperson for few weeks, and compensated for landing my name and my persona to their promotion.

When you get to the point in your blogging career where brands approach you for deals using your brand, make sure to hire an agent or at least a lawyer to help you navigate through the complex dynamics of a spokesperson deal.

- **Develop a line of products.** Another way of common brand collaboration is through your very own line of products, created under the larger brand's umbrella of consumer offerings. It makes sense to join forces even with a smaller brand, because they will be able to provide the necessary infrastructure for the production of your product. Whether it's a shoe or a jewelry line with your name on it, make sure you get a cut of the sales generated from your products, so you have an incentive to promote the line.

Don't be afraid to approach your favorite brands with ideas and initiate such collaborations—you will be surprised how open brands are to creative ideas involving influencers. Again, if you can show your potential value to the brand, you can sell them on even the most outrageous ideas.

- **Write a book.** It might look like everyone is writing a book these days, and it's somewhat true. Online self-publishing tools are so accessible and easy that pretty much everyone can have a book published with a little dedication and effort.

I decided to publish this book after writing a few posts on my blog and realizing there might be value in my advice, that some of my readers might be even willing to pay for my "packaged advice." Even if you write about a certain subject every day, there is a value in the content being packaged, edited and well-formatted in a way your readers can digest all at once. After deciding on my book's subject, I realized about twenty percent of my content was already written in different parts and posts on my blog, which provided a great start for the book. From there, it was just expanding and enriching content, which took a total of five months to accomplish—not a long time for a book, considering I wrote mostly during nights and weekends.

Books are a great way to sell your knowledge, which is still hard to monetize online. Your readers get free access to your content on a daily basis while you spend hours of your time crafting every blog post and perfecting your writing. The good news is that people are still willing to pay for a good book, so think about what kind of book will add value to your readers and will help positioning your further as an expert of your domain.

These are just some of the ideas for additional revenue streams you can create from your blog. The possibilities are endless, so it's up to you to come up with which ideas and formats work best. As long as you have a revenue strategy, every project that supports your financial goals is worth your time and effort. Get your entrepreneurial juices flowing and come up with unique ideas and formats that work for you. You don't have to compromise your voice to become well-compensated doing something you love. After all, that's the whole point of this book.

Blogger Inspiration: Q&A with Zephyr Basine of CollegeFashion.

How did you come up with the name and the focus for your blog?

I first had the idea for College Fashion in late 2006, when I was a 19-year-old college sophomore. At the time, fashion blogging was just starting to take off. At the same time, I began to notice that none of my favorite fashion websites or magazines catered to my demographic of college students. There was tons of content out there for high school students and 30-year-old women with high incomes, but absolutely nothing for the girls in between.

As a marketing and business major, I was always seeking business opportunities and thought a fashion site aimed at college students had a lot of potential. On a whim, I decided since no one had created a fashion site for college girls, I'd start one myself. College Fashion was a natural choice of title, so I registered the domain name right away. Fortunately, I already had lots of HTML and graphic design experience (teenage nerds represent!), so I built the site from scratch over winter break, and launched it on March 1st, 2007.

From there, the site grew fast and by March of 2008, CF was receiving an average of 30,000 unique visitors per month, and by March 2009, traffic had increased 400%, to 150,000 visitors per month. What's funny, however, is that I didn't employ any special tactics to promote the site. In fact, I'd say 99% of College Fashion's growth has been organic—readers find CF content through Google or links on other sites and tell their friends about the site, those friends check the site out and tell their friends, and it went from there.

How did you build your audience?

Instead of working to publicize the site, I chose to focus on what I now believe is **the key** to a successful blog: creating high quality content. I have spent hours painstakingly crafting each post, making sure every image looked perfect, every word was spelled correctly, and every paragraph was brimming with useful, relevant information for our target audience. I often skipped class so I could finish polishing a 1,000 word post—I was that obsessed. This focus on quality content, combined with the blog's unique concept, is what I believe made CF such a success.

Is there one piece of advice you can give to aspiring professional bloggers?

If I could give one piece of advice to aspiring pro bloggers, it's this: be original. By now, most of the "obvious" blog topics have been taken and done to death. There are thousands of well-established sites out there on every topic imaginable, and most of them have had a five-year head start. You would have to be crazy to create a copycat site today and expect to compete with any of them.

In my opinion, the only way to really succeed with a new blog today is to come up with a topic that's outside-the-box and to do something that no one else has done. You don't have to reinvent the wheel, of course, but you do need to be creative—you will never succeed by copying someone else's blog topic or style. On the other hand, you will garner respect from other bloggers and get people talking if you come up with something that they haven't seen before.

What about one good warning for aspiring professional bloggers?

One word of warning I'd like to give aspiring pro bloggers: Don't spam people! Although as I mentioned earlier, 99% of College Fashion's growth has been organic, during my first months of blogging, I read those "blogging tip" sites and foolishly attempted to promote my blog using their tactics. This was probably my biggest blogging mistake, and something I definitely wish I could take back.

After a few weeks of blogging, as directed by a post on "Ten Ways to Promote Your Blog", I emailed a bunch of fashion bloggers I admired, asking if they'd check out my site and if they would like to exchange links. Predictably, none of them got back to me.

At first, I was confused as to why no one responded. After all, my blog topic was totally unique! I was writing great content! Everyone who visited my site seemed to love it! Fortunately, I didn't dwell on this for long, and gave up after the first round of unanswered emails: I can't imagine the damage I could have done to my blog's reputation had I continued.

Today I receive at least one link exchange request per day, and I now understand why no one answered my emails: 99% of link exchange requests are one-sided. If you're a new blogger mass-emailing established blogs for links, you're essentially cold calling people you don't know and asking for favors, without offering anything in return. In short, you come off desperate, inconsiderate and rude—not exactly the best way to start off in the blogging community.

So, if you're a new blogger starting out, resist the urge to send everyone and their mom a link to your blog, and don't ask random bloggers for link exchanges, at least until your site is very well-established or you have a strong relationship with said blogger. Take it from me: these tactics can be the quickest way to alienate the very people you want to network with the most.

What are some of the revenue channels for your blog?

Whenever I talk about blogging for money, I always make sure to mention one thing first: blogging is **not** a "get rich quick" scheme by any stretch of the imagination! Although College Fashion is profitable today, I basically worked for free for two years before I saw any real income from the site, and most blogs take longer than that to become profitable.

Trust me when I say there are *much* easier and faster ways to make money if that's all you're after!

As a business major, I've always understood it was possible to make money from blogging, so while College Fashion was mostly a hobby in the beginning, I started experimenting with ads early, and always knew that blogging could someday become my full-time job.

Over the years, I experimented with many different types of revenue streams on CF, beginning with Google AdSense and moving to affiliate networks like Commission Junction, contextual search ad networks like Chitika, private ad sales, and eventually larger ad networks like Glam, and finally Style Coalition.

As I mentioned above, however, I didn't see much income from CF until early 2009. So when I graduated from college in May of that year, I was faced with a choice: shut down College Fashion and get a "real job," or keep the site going and work on it full-time in hopes that it would continue to make enough money to cover my (minimal) living expenses. I weighed the pros and cons with my boyfriend and we came up with a plan: I would take the next year off and work full-time on the site, and if after one year I didn't want to do it anymore, or the site wasn't doing as well as I had hoped, I'd reevaluate and, if necessary, move on.

Of course, after 12 months, I found myself at the helm of a successful, profitable business. College Fashion was more popular than ever, our traffic numbers were rising every month, and I couldn't imagine giving up my self-employed lifestyle to work in someone else's office. That sealed the deal: I'm now a professional blogger and I absolutely love it.

What kind of opportunities have opened up for you as a full time blogger that you could not have done before?

Today, College Fashion receives nearly one million unique visitors per month from over 200 countries and territories, and our traffic numbers are constantly growing. We've collaborated on giveaways and promotions with brands including Victoria's Secret, Microsoft, Lancôme, HP, Coca Cola, MTV, JCPenney, Target, Reebok, Juicy Couture, and many more. And blogging has its personal perks: I've attended New York Fashion Week three times, traveled all over the country for events, sat at runway shows, and interviewed celebrities—all in a few short years.

Many of these amazing opportunities simply popped up in my inbox. When you work to build a unique, interesting, helpful blog that readers love, people notice and they want to work with you. While many bloggers actively "pitch" reporters and PR people, I've found that the best opportunities tend to be those I don't actively seek out.

Overall, I couldn't be happier with my decision to "go pro" at blogging instead of "getting a job." While it was definitely a risk (both financially and career-wise), the benefits of owning my own business have certainly outweighed the costs. Today, I get to do what I love and get paid for it and, to me, it just doesn't get better than that.

Action Items.

- Install Google Analytics and follow your reports closely. Create a short report at the end of each month, including such statistics as which keywords bring the most traffic, which sites refer most of your readers, where your readers are located, and which of your posts are most successful. Document and compare these learnings every month to keep track of what works and what doesn't.

- Quantify your site using Quantcast's code to start collecting your demographic data.

- Research editorial guidelines on other blogs and come up with your own version, the one with which you feel most comfortable.

- Sign up for one of the affiliate networks and experiment with affiliate links in one of your posts. Keep checking the stats and adjust your strategy accordingly.

- Make a list of unique revenue opportunities you can create with your blog: special features that could be sponsored, workshops or other services you could offer based on your blog's focus, or an online store where you could sell your own products. Focus on one that excites you most and make a plan to develop it in the next year.

- Research the going market rate by asking other bloggers and marketing professionals on their rates. Decide upon your own rates based on these findings and the monetary amounts you are most comfortable requesting.

- Collect the data for your Media Kit and put it into a simple PowerPoint document. Upload it to your blog, so you can easily send it to potential clients via a simple link.

Helpful Resources

Blog Hosting Sites:

www.wordpress.com - The most popular of blogging platforms, WordPress can be easily customized (with a little bit of advanced knowledge). It's known for looking professional and having many formatting options.

Note: please be aware of the differences between WordPress.com and WordPress.org! As stated in the WordPress' Help section, "WordPress.com is a hosted blog service. You do not have to download software, pay for hosting or manage a web server. WordPress.com does not permit uploading themes or plug-ins. WordPress.org is free software. You can install themes and plug-ins, run ads, and edit the database."

www.tumblr.com - Tumblr is a trendy microblogging platform known for its ease of use and highly visual aesthetic. Users can post text, images, videos, links, quotes and audio to their "tumblelog." The feature that stands out on Tumblr is the near-instant publishing capability and social aspect. Editing your theme is possible, but limited to a few specific layouts.

Of course, there are many other options for blog hosting, but the ones above are what I would suggest for professional and serious bloggers.

Claiming Your Domain Name:

www.godaddy.com - Go Daddy is a domain registration service and web hosting company. Here you can buy and manage your own domain names.

CSS, HTML, and Coding Help:

www.html.net - Visit this website for a basic step-by-guide to html, CSS, and coding.

Blog Design:

Go to your local art schools and universities. Often there are students willing to do a project for the experience or a low cost.

www.aiga.org - Click "Find a Designer" here to find a professional graphic designer or a student designer who will work for discounted rates.

www.freelance.com - A simple-to-use website for reaching out and finding professional freelancers. Post your job or a project and the free service will act as the middleman to find a designer.

www.taskarmy.com - An outsourcing service with a satisfaction guarantee. Search for a service and choose from the various offers at a range of prices.

www.Vistaprint.com - Vistaprint is constantly running a promotion where you can get a large amount of premium and professional looking business cards for a very low cost, sometimes even with free shipping.

www.4by6.com - This is a creative and high-quality card design website with especially beautiful paper. You can apply to receive a free sample kit before making any print jobs.

Branding:

www.brandyourself.com - a great online tool for managing the online exposure you get from Google, eliminating the negative and only showing positive links about you.

Deckers, Erik, and Kyle Lacy. *Branding Yourself: How to Use Social Media To Invent or Reinvent Yourself.* Indianapolis, IN. (Que Pub., 2011) Print. This book contains tips on how to build your own personal brand through the proper use of social media.

Business Plan Resources:

www.inc.com/start-up - Inc. is a really great resource for any type of business advice, especially the business plan outline.

Legal Language:

www.dictionary.law.com - Law dictionary to look up legal terms by word or definition.

www.eff.org/issues/bloggers - The Electronic Frontier Foundation has a page specifically on the Rights of Bloggers. It outlines important legal issues bloggers should know about and can answer many questions you might have.

Business Etiquette:

www.emilypost.com - A useful site with lots of advice on proper business etiquette from proper dress to manners and international customs. Extremely important for the serious business person.

Post, Peggy, and Peter Post. *Emily Post's The Etiquette Advantage in Business: Personal Skills for Professional Success, Second.* 2nd ed. (William Morrow, 2005). Print. A more thorough companion book to the website and an excellent reference manual, this is a must-have for the serious business person.

Classes and Workshops:

www.cuny.edu - If you are a New York state resident, find a NY state school to take individual classes for a reasonable price. If not, look for local classes you can take through your local college or university system.

www.fitnyc.edu - Find continuing education classes in a variety of fashion disciplines.

www.limcollege.edu - Find classes taught on the business of fashion.

www.skillshare.com - Find local workshops on a variety of subjects, and even offer your own!

Writing Skills:

www.writingclasses.com - Gotham Writers Workshop offers in person and online classes on different topics, including "How to Blog."

www.problogger.net - Problogger is great a website full of blogging tips, from finding your voice to choosing the right layout for your site.

www.bloggingpro.com - This website has tons of tips on branding your blog, including setting goals, guest blogging, consistency and design.

www.lifehack.com - A good resource for self-improvement, including a page with 63 points of simple advice on building confidence within yourself and as a writer.

Visuals for your blog:

www.creativecommons.org - Here you can find all the information you need to know about what Creative Commons are and how they work.

www.flickr.com - Using the Creative Commons option on a Flickr search will result in a list of photos that have a creative commons license. Flickr can explain further how to use them.

Photography:

www.icp.org - The International Center of Photography offers various courses, seminars, and workshops on using DSLR, photography techniques, editing, and blog photography.

www.advancedphotography.net - This website has tips for choosing the best camera for you and some advice on professional photography.

www.howtogeek.com - This how-to website has a great 8-part article on the basics of Photoshop and how to use all of its components. You can find many other guides for technical tasks here, as well.

Networking:

www.meetup.com - Find a meet-up event in fashion or technology in your area. These events are fantastic places to meet contacts and expand your network with professionals.

www.eventbrite.com - Find popular events in your area, as well as manage and promote an event you're planning yourself.

www.heartifb.com - Independent Fashion Bloggers is a blogging community for fashion bloggers to connect and share resources.

New York Fashion Week:

www.mbfashionweek.com/press - use the registration form to apply for press credentials as early as possible, up to two months in advance when registration opens.

www.modemonline.com - Modem Online supplies vital information, like schedules of shows and presentations, indexes of brands, showrooms, and their PR contacts.

Editorial Guidelines:

Examples of great "Blog Guidelines" pages:

www.stylebakery.com/disclosures.html

www.prettyshinysparkly.com/about/disclosure-policy

www.grechenscloset.com/editorial-policy

Measure and Collect Your Data:

www.google.com/analytics - Google Analytics has an easy explanations and set up, and this page will supply all the information you may need.

www.googlekeywordtool.com - Use Google Keywords to find out the most searched-for terms, including how much estimated traffic you will get by using certain words.

www.quantcast.com - Quantcast will find out the demographics of your readers just by entering your domain address. Get Quantified for more accurate info.

www.alexa.com - Use Alexa to get an idea of how much traffic your competitors are gaining in comparison to yours.

www.feedburner.google.com - FeedBurner can set up RSS feeds to make reading your blog easy for your subscribers.

Advertising terms:

www.iab.net/iab_products_and_industry_services - the IAB can provide guidelines and best practices for placing ads.

Media Kits:

For examples of how to create a media kit, check out these websites:

www.heartifb.com/2010/01/15/media-kit

www.stylesamplemag.com

www.thecurvyfashionista.mariedenee.com/Media-Kit.pdf

End Notes.

Thank you for joining me on this journey, the process of perfecting the art and business of blogging. From making a plan to creating your identity, building valuable relationships and eventually monetizing your efforts. I hope you've experienced some sort of transformation while reading, either in your thoughts or actions. I would love to hear your stories, questions and feedback via my website, *YuliZiv.com*, or via Twitter, *@yuliz.*

Writing this book made me aware of how satisfying the process of putting my thoughts on paper (or a computer screen) can be, so I'm sure this won't be my last book. The accessibility of self-publishing today gives everyone with an idea for a story or a book the ability to become an author, and I'm thankful to live in this age, one full of possibilities.

I hope to continue the Fashion 2.0 book series and share more thoughts on this fast-paced, newly-developing space. Perhaps I will be lucky to share some of your stories in the upcoming books. After all, there is nothing I want more than for each one of you, my readers, to succeed and fulfill your purpose.

The highest honor I can receive is your success. So, here's to your success as a blogger.

Until next time,

Yuli Ziv

Acknowledgements.

Many people contributed to the knowledge I share in this book. I would like to thank all of the Style Coalition bloggers for the opportunity to work with them over the past few years, and especially to those who contributed their guest chapters to this book: *Kat Griffin, Gala Darling, Lauren Dimet-Waters, Jessica Quirk* and *Zephyr Basine*. Your dedication to your craft and the professionalism you project are truly inspiring.

Thank you to my amazing partners at *ELLE, Ted Nadeau* and *Jonas Abney,* who gave our blogging network the opportunity of a lifetime and opened the door to possibilities we've never even dreamed of.

Thank you to my book editor, *Kristin Booker,* whose passionate feedback kept me writing every free minute I've had for the past five months, including nights and weekends. You've made my foreign accent much less noticeable in this book.

Thank you to my dear friend, *Julia DiNardo,* for spending a sleepless night reviewing the book and to my dedicated assistants *Christine Ongsueng* and *Elysia Mann,* for the research of helpful resources, feedback and help. Thanks to the most talented photographer *Ana Schechter* for making me feel special on this book cover, and thanks to my publicist *Courtney Forrest* for believing in me.

I couldn't have done it without my parents, who raised me as an over-achiever from an early age, which I find to an important quality for a first time author. I would like to thank my brother, who's been my life coach for these challenging last few years.

Lastly, thank you, *Yanni.* You've been my rock and my biggest source of inspiration this year. I love you.

CPSIA information can be obtained at www.ICGtesting.com
Printed in the USA
LVOW01s2131181113

361791LV00024B/1422/P